The Encyclopedia of Drugs and Alcohol

The Encyclopedia of Drugs and Alcohol

Written by Greg Roza

Franklin Watts
a Division of Scholastic Inc.
New York • Toronto • London
Auckland • Sydney • Mexico City
New Delhi • Hong Kong • Danbury, CT

Published in 2001 by The Rosen Publishing Group, Inc.
29 East 21st Street, New York, NY 10010

First Edition

Library of Congress Cataloging-in-Publication Data

Roza, Greg.
    The encyclopedia of drugs and alcohol/Greg Roza.
       p. cm.
    Includes bibliographical references and index.
    ISBN 0-531-11899-1
       1. Drugs—Encyclopedias—Juvenile literature. 2. Drugs of abuse—Encyclopedias—Juvenile literature. [1. Drugs—Encyclopedias. 2. Drug abuse—Encyclopedias.] I. Title.

RM301.17 .R698 2001
615'.1'03—dc21   00-045913

Table of Contents

Introduction

Statistics for 1999 show that, in general, illicit drug use among high school students over the previous three years remained stable or declined (National Institute on Drug Abuse study, *Monitoring the Future*). This is great news, right? A reason to celebrate?

Not so fast. Surface statistics can be misleading. For instance, while statistics show that monthly marijuana use among twelfth graders has remained stable since 1997 at about 23 percent, marijuana use among tenth graders is slightly higher. Teen use of cigarettes has been declining since 1996, but 1999 statistics report that 15.9 percent of tenth graders and 23.1 percent of twelfth graders smoke cigarettes daily. Furthermore, while the use of many illicit drugs appears to be on the decline, it is obvious that other drugs—particularly alcohol, anabolic steroids, and MDMA (ecstasy)—are steadily becoming more and more popular with teens.

Again one must ask this question: Are these findings truly a reason to celebrate the effects of the "war on drugs"? Should we be content simply because statistics show that the monthly use of inhalants among twelfth graders is down to 5.6 percent, when monthly inhalant use for eighth graders is at 10.3 percent? And isn't 5.6 percent of America's twelfth graders inhaling dangerous, life-threatening chemicals still a reason for concern? Furthermore, drug abuse is not only a problem with illicit drugs. Some studies report that over half of drug-related emergency room cases are caused by prescription drug use and overdose ("Prescription Drug Use and Abuse." *Psychiatric Times*, Vol XII, No.1, January 1995).

The point is this: Statistics may claim that drug use is declining, remaining stable, or increasing, but the bottom line is that substance abuse and teen drug use are still problems in the United States. Drug use will remain a major problem until youthful Americans are helped to fully understand the dangers associated with drugs, illegal as well as legal. Education about the risks of drug use is the first step in reducing these statistics to a more acceptable percentage: zero.

The book you hold in your hands is a guide to common drugs: prescription, over-the-counter, and recreational—the extremely dangerous and the seemingly harmless. While simply knowing more about the dangers of drugs and the drugs themselves won't make you impervious to substance abuse, it will help you to make informed, educated decisions about drug use.

Not all drugs are harmful to you. In fact, some drugs—like antibiotics and analgesics—are beneficial to many people on a daily basis. All drugs, however, can become dangerous when abused—that is, when used in a manner not recommended by a doctor—or when dosage instructions are ignored. Don't allow a lack of knowledge to turn you into just another statistic. Use this book to arm yourself with the knowledge to use the drugs you need correctly and to wisely avoid the drugs that can only hurt you.

A

- Abstinence
- Acetaminophen
- Acid
- Addiction
- Addictive
  Personality
- Adrenaline
- Adulterant
- Aerosol
- AIDS
- Akyl Nitrite
- Al-Anon
- Alcohol
- Alcoholics
  Anonymous
- Alcoholism
- Alcohol
  Poisoning
- Amphetamine
- Amyl Nitrite
- Amytal
- Anabolic
  Steroid
- Analgesic
- Anemia
- Anesthetic
- Antabuse
- Antacid
- Antianxiety
  Drug
- Antibiotic
- Antidepressant
- Antidote
- Antifungal Drug
- Antihistamine
- Antipsychotic
  Drug
- Antiviral Drug
- Aspirin
- AZT

See also:
Temperance

Abstinence

Complete avoidance of an activity. Abstinence is more than simply avoiding an excess of an activity; it is the absence of the activity altogether. Abstinence is a crucial part of many *drug recovery* programs.

Abstinence from *alcohol* was the goal of the *prohibition* movement in the United States. In 1920, the movement achieved the ratification of the Eighteenth Amendment to the Constitution, which prohibited the sale of alcohol. This amendment was so widely ignored that it was repealed thirteen years later in the Twenty-first Amendment to the Constitution.

Abstinence is also a key term in *drug rehabilitation*. People who become addicted to a substance have a compulsion to use it regardless of the consequences. When in recovery, abstinence allows the user to rid his or her system of the drug and to fight the compulsion to use other drugs instead. In many cases, abstinence is the only way to achieve a completely healthy system after having used drugs for an extended period of time. Abstinence is at the center of *twelve-step programs,* such as *Alcoholics Anonymous*, which help people to help themselves in reaching *sobriety.*

Acetaminophen

An *over-the-counter drug* used for relieving pain and lowering fever. This drug is comparable to, but lacks the anti-inflammatory ability of, *aspirin* and *ibuprofen.*

Although it is not known how acetaminophen works, it is used successfully for relieving some symptoms of colds, allergies, and physical injuries. New research shows it to be beneficial in blocking the pain associated with arthritis (inflammation of a joint) and osteoarthritis (degeneration of joint cartilage). Unlike aspirin and ibuprofen, acetaminophen has little or no adverse effect on the stomach.

Taking large *doses* of acetaminophen over long periods of time can lead to *kidney* disease. A dose as large as fifteen grams or more can produce irreversible *liver* damage, especially for people who drink *alcohol* regularly. People should be careful not to use too many products containing acetaminophen at one time (cold medicines, allergy remedies, pain relievers) to avoid acetaminophen *poisoning,* which can lead to death.

Acid

See *LSD.*

Addiction

An unhealthy obsession with a certain activity or substance. *Drug abuse* and *alcoholism* are common forms of addiction. An addiction is caused by repeated participation in an activity until it becomes a harmful fixation in one's daily life, or by using a particular substance so often that it becomes difficult to live without that substance's effect. Addiction to *drugs* and *alcohol* manifests in two ways: *psychological dependence* and *physical dependence*.

Addiction, especially in the case of drug and alcohol abuse, can cause one's physical well-being to deteriorate over a period of time. Negative health effects can include *heart* disease, *liver* and *kidney* disease, *lung* disease, nervous disorders, and even death. Addiction can also affect one's ability to work, go to school, interact with family and friends, and carry out everyday activities.

Addictions manifest in a wide variety of people from all walks of life. It is not exactly clear how addictions develop, but they can be initiated by a number of factors, including social pressure, personality, and availability of the substance or activity. Also, it is believed that chemicals in the brain, such as norepinephrine, are different in people with addictions. Some researchers believe addictions may be hereditary. Treatment for addictions include family *intervention, drug rehabilitation* programs, psychological counseling, and medical attention.

Addiction to drugs and/or alcohol can lead to physical and psychological deterioration.

Addictive Personality

The compulsion to behave in a way that is harmful to one's well-being. An addictive person often has more than one *addiction (cross-drug addiction)*, works to hide these addictions from others, and allows the addictions to affect relationships with family and friends, work, school, and other areas of everyday life. Detrimental factors that go hand-in-hand with an addictive personality include *depression,* low self-esteem, nervousness, impulsive actions, and difficulty in coping with everyday life.

When associated with substance abuse, addictive personalities exhibit common characteristics. People addicted to *drugs* and/or *alcohol* develop a *tolerance* for the substance and experience *withdrawal* symptoms when they try to quit using it. They spend excessive time and money using the drugs

to which they are addicted and often begin using other drugs. What follow are ineffectual efforts to quit using, extreme usage, and a reduced participation in society. They continue to use the drug despite knowing that it is harmful and despite repeated warnings from people close to them.

The first step in coping with an addictive personality is ending the habitual presence of the object or event. It is equally important to become familiar with one's addictive tendencies and to rid oneself of addictive behaviors. These goals can be attained with the aid of alcohol and *drug rehabilitation*, a *twelve-step program*, and the help of friends and family.

Adrenaline

A hormone secreted by the adrenal glands, which are located above the *kidneys.* Adrenaline is another name for the hormone epinephrine. Adrenaline allows the body to respond to sudden stress. When a person becomes frightened, threatened, injured, or angry, the brain sends a signal to the adrenal glands, which in turn release adrenaline into the system. Adrenaline increases *heart* and breathing rates, raises blood pressure, creates extra glucose (a type of sugar made by the body for energy), and slows the process of digestion to allow more blood to go to the muscles. This reaction is often referred to as "fight or flight" because it prepares the body for immediate action.

Adrenaline is made *synthetically* for medical purposes. It is used to treat shock, to restore the heartbeat of patients suffering *cardiac arrest,* to prevent bleeding, and (in the form of mist inhalers) to treat respiratory problems such as asthma and croup.

Certain *drugs,* such as *amphetamines,* increase the amount of adrenaline that the adrenal glands release into the body. This can result in heightened alertness, physical performance, and mental activity, as well as inability to sleep and decreased appetite.

Adulterant

A *psychoactive drug* added to another drug to mimic its effects. This is primarily done by *dealers* who want to increase their *drug* supply and thus their profits. For example, *caffeine* and *ephedrine* are often added to certain *amphetamines* because they have similar effects on the body. Drug users usually cannot tell the difference. Researchers have discovered that many illegal drugs—particularly amphetamines, *cocaine,* and *heroin*—are almost always mixed with other substances. These impurities make such drugs even more dangerous because one never knows exactly what one is taking.

Aerosol

A mixture of tiny particles and gas dispensed from a pressurized container. Products like deodorant and hair spray are sometimes sold in aerosol form.

Aerosol sprays—most notably spray paint and air fresheners—are abused as *inhalants* to achieve a *high*. Aerosol products contain fluorocarbons (also found in refrigerators and air conditioners), which act to propel the product from its container. Some aerosols also contain butane (cigarette lighter fluid) and propane. The effects of inhaling these chemicals are usually short-lived but can sometimes last up to an hour.

People who inhale aerosols often spray them into a paper bag or into a cloth to concentrate the substance. The aerosol is then deeply inhaled.

AIDS

See also:
Volatile Solvent

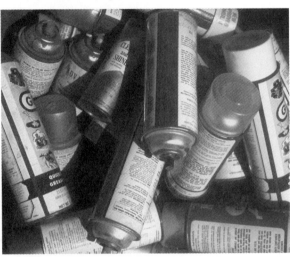

Aerosol products such as spray paint are sometimes inhaled for a short-term high.

AIDS

Acquired immunodeficiency syndrome, the breakdown of the human body's *immune system* because of HIV, or human immunodeficiency virus. HIV is commonly transmitted through unprotected sexual activity or when *drug* users share needles used to *inject* drugs into the body. As the effects of HIV worsen, the person becomes unable to fight off infections that would not normally be life-threatening. These infections are called opportunistic because they prey on weakened immune systems and arise from organisms that normally live on the body. As these infections appear with increasing regularity, the person is said to have AIDS.

A person can be diagnosed HIV-positive and not develop AIDS for two to fifteen years, or longer. Once HIV develops into AIDS, however, the person can quickly contract any number of opportunistic infections. The typical symptoms of AIDS include swollen lymph nodes, weight loss, fever, fatigue, diarrhea, *anemia,* and thrush (infection of the mouth).

The leading cause of death among AIDS patients is Pneumocystis carinii pneumonia, an infection of the lungs. AIDS patients can also develop one or more of the following: Kaposi's sarcoma (skin disease), *tuberculosis,* cytomegalovirus.retinitis (an eye infection that can lead to blindness), or progressive multifocal leukoencephalopathy (a viral infection of the brain).

As yet, there is no cure for AIDS. Certain prescribed drugs can help prevent infections—particularly sulfamethoxazole and trimethoprim (Bactrim)—but none is 100 percent effective.

See also:
HIV

Akyl Nitrite

A yellow, flammable liquid misused as an *inhalant.* Akyl nitrites have a sweet odor and are commonly found in liquid air fresheners. *Amyl nitrite* and *butyl nitrite* are two types of akyl nitrite.

Inhaling akyl nitrites produces a lightheaded feeling, or *high,* which usually lasts no longer than two minutes. Unlike most inhalants—which act as *depressants*—akyl nitrites act as *stimulants,* speeding up the *heart* rate. They dilate the blood vessels, allowing more blood to reach the heart. Other effects may include a flushed sensation, increased sensory awareness, headache, dizziness, nausea, coughing, and *blackout.* Although inhaling akyl nitrites has not been proven to cause *sudden sniffing death,* deaths due to ingestion have been documented.

There is no evidence that akyl nitrites cause *physical dependence,* but they can cause *psychological dependence.* Use of them often builds a *tolerance* to their ability to dilate the blood vessels, but there is no evidence to support the idea of tolerance to the stimulative effects.

Some consider akyl nitrites *club drugs,* and they are often combined with *amphetamines* and *ecstasy* to increase their effects. Akyl nitrites are also used as sexual stimulants because they enhance pleasure by affecting the amount of oxygen that reaches the brain. New research has shown that akyl nitrites may be linked with *immune system* deficiencies.

Al-Anon

A voluntary self-help group for the relatives of alcoholics. People attend Al-Anon meetings to discuss the difficulties and dangers of living with an alcoholic. Al-Anon, and a similar group called Alateen, are patterned after *twelve-step programs,* which alcoholics themselves follow. Many of the people who attend Al-Anon meetings exhibit the symptoms of a *codependent* personality. Sharing problems helps to build an understanding of *alcoholism* as a disease, teaches people how to deal with alcoholic relatives, and builds feelings of self-worth. Founded in the 1930s, Al-Anon is now a worldwide organization.

Alcohol

An *intoxicating* beverage that contains ethanol (ethyl alcohol). Alcoholic beverages are made primarily from grains and fruits. There are two types of alcohol: *fermented alcohol* and *distilled alcohol.*

Alcohol enters the blood through the small intestines and is metabolized by the *liver.* Brain function is depressed as alcohol reaches the brain through the bloodstream. The level of impairment depends on how much alcohol is in the blood.

Alcohol is a *depressant.* It numbs the nervous system, producing a relaxing effect in the user. Small amounts may act as a *stimulant,* resulting in talkativeness, loss of inhibitions, mood swings, and emotional outbursts. Physical effects include slurred speech, loss of coordination, and impaired balance. Large amounts of alcohol can cause memory loss, *depression, blackout, coma,* and death.

Prolonged, excessive alcohol consumption can lead to *alcoholism* as well as other severe illnesses, such as *anemia,* ulcers, *cardiac arrhythmia, heart failure, hypertension, stroke,* nerve damage, brain damage, *hepatitis, cirrhosis of the liver,* and *cancers* of the *liver,* pancreas, and esophagus. Long-term use of alcohol can permanently damage organs of the body, particularly the brain, liver, and *heart.*

Alcohol is used in many situations by many different types of people. As a legal *drug,* alcohol is widely accepted in social settings and is consumed at public and private events, celebrations, and in sites especially established for its consumption (bars, clubs). Alcohol can become highly addictive, however, and some people find themselves drinking many times throughout the day, even when they are at work or school and while they are alone. *DWI* (driving while intoxicated) is a particularly destructive problem in modern society.

See also:
Alcohol Poisoning
Blood Alcohol Level

Alcohol abuse is the cause of many illnesses, including cancer and cirrhosis of the liver.

Alcoholics Anonymous

See *Twelve-Step Program.*

Alcoholism

A disease distinguished by the inability to stop drinking *alcohol.* Alcoholism is one of the most common forms of *addiction;* approximately 8 percent of adults in the United States have alcohol problems.

Although the cause of alcoholism is unclear, researchers believe many factors are involved, including personality, family background, and even genetics. Alcoholism affects every area of a person's life: physical and mental health, family and social relationships, and professional or educational careers. Normally enjoyed socially, alcohol takes over the alcoholic's life, and he or she drinks several times a day, at all times of the day, even when alone.

Alcohol produces both *psychological* and *physical dependence* in long-term users. Alcoholics develop a *tolerance* for alcohol. When they stop drinking, they often experience *withdrawal* symptoms, which range in severity from tremors and nausea to *seizures* and *hallucinations.* If alcohol withdrawal is untreated, it can deteriorate into a condition known as *delirium tremens.*

Alcohol rehabilitation begins with medical attention for the withdrawal symptoms. *Detoxification* can include large *doses* of vitamins B and C, *benzodiazepines,* and, sometimes, *antipsychotic drugs* to reduce hallucinations. Delirium tremens requires close medical supervision and is usually treated with sedatives and *acetaminophen.* After the withdrawal symptoms are relieved, rehabilitation may include psychological testing, counseling, and family therapy sessions. Certain *drugs* may be used to help alcoholics remain *sober,* including *Antabuse* and *naltrexone.* Many alcoholics have benefited from attending *Alcoholics Anonymous* meetings.

Alcohol Poisoning

A condition that develops from drinking a large amount of *alcohol* in a short time. It is marked by a lack of response to physical stimuli; inability to stand, walk, and talk clearly; slow or abnormal breathing; purple, clammy skin; *cardiac arrhythmia; low blood pressure;* and *heart failure.* Alcohol poisoning can result in unconsciousness and *coma.* People with alcohol poisoning sometimes choke on their own vomit.

Alcohol poisoning can occur when the *blood alcohol level* is around .30 percent, but it can happen at lower or higher levels depending on the

See also:
Alcohol
Alcoholism
Twelve-Step Program

person. Alcohol poisoning requires immediate medical attention. Treatment usually includes emptying the contents of the stomach to avoid further alcohol digestion.

Alcohol poisoning most often happens to people who are *binge drinkers*. Many of these cases result in death.

Amphetamine

A type of *stimulant* that affects the *central nervous system*. Amphetamines are *synthetic drugs* that speed up the body for four to six hours by increasing the amount of *adrenaline* in the body. Amphetamines can be taken orally, *injected*, or *snorted*.

Amphetamines are commonly prescribed for three reasons: as an appetite suppressant, for patients with narcolepsy (sudden daytime sleep), and for children with attention deficit hyperactivity disorder (ADHD), a brain disorder marked by constant activity and lack of concentration. For reasons unknown to scientists, amphetamines have an opposite effect on children with hyperkinesis than they do on others.

Amphetamines increase alertness and physical performance, heighten mental activity, hinder sleep, and decrease appetite. Other short-term effects include talkativeness, aggressiveness, increased breathing and *heart rate*, *hallucinations*, *euphoria*, mood swings, blurred vision, loss of coordination, and unconsciousness. People who use amphetamines experience extreme *depression* when the *high* wears off (known as a *crash*). Amphetamine abuse can also cause death from burst blood vessels in the brain, *heart failure*, *stroke*, or very high fever.

Long-term effects include paranoid schizophrenia, malnutrition, increased susceptibility to illness, and blocked blood vessels. People who inject amphetamines also risk contracting *HIV* from infected needles.

This type of drug is often taken illegally for a number of reasons. Some people take amphetamines to excel in athletics, whereas others take them to stay awake. Amphetamines like *methamphetamine* and *MDMA* are taken strictly for their euphoric effects.

Addiction to amphetamines can happen quickly, and users frequently build a *tolerance* for them. Persons addicted to amphetamines may experience both *psychological* and *physical dependence*. *Withdrawal* symptoms include severe exhaustion, long periods of sleep, extreme hunger, depression, anxiety, and psychotic reactions. *Drug rehabilitation* includes *detoxification*, counseling, and *twelve-step programs*.

See also:
Club Drug

Amyl Nitrite

See also:
Akyl Nitrite
Hypnotic-Sedative

Amyl Nitrite

A yellow, flammable liquid commonly misused as an *inhalant*. Amyl nitrite can be found in a number of liquid air fresheners and is prescribed for various circulatory diseases. As an inhalant, it is known as a "popper" because it was once manufactured in glass vials that were broken (or popped) open and then inhaled.

Unlike most inhalants—which act as *depressants*—amyl nitrite acts as a *stimulant,* speeding up the *heart* rate. It dilates the blood vessels, allowing more blood to reach the heart. Other effects may include a flushed sensation, increased sensory awareness, headache, dizziness, nausea, coughing, and *blackout.*

Amyl nitrite is sometimes prescribed for persons with coronary artery disease (obstruction of blood flow due to fatty deposits in the coronary artery) and angina pectoris (lack of oxygen to the heart due to constricted blood vessels) because it increases heart rate and lowers blood pressure. For the same reasons, amyl nitrite should be avoided by people who have *anemia* or *hypertension* and by women who are pregnant. It is used as an aphrodisiac (sexual stimulant) and is often sold illegally in sex shops. Amyl nitrite is also considered a *club drug* and is often used to heighten the effects of *amphetamines* and *MDMA,* or *ecstasy.*

Amytal

A *barbiturate;* a *prescription drug* used primarily to treat sleeplessness, but also anxiety, tension, *hypertension,* and convulsions. It is sometimes used as an *anesthetic.* This *drug* can be taken orally in pill form or *injected.*

Like all barbiturates, Amytal slows the *central nervous system.* Small *doses* can relieve tension, but large doses can cause blurred vision, impaired thinking, staggering, slurred speech, impaired perception, slowed reflexes and breathing, and reduced sensitivity to pain. Long-term effects of prolonged use can include *anemia, liver* damage, and *depression.*

People who take Amytal regularly can develop a *tolerance* for the drug. Accidental *overdose* can occur when people who have developed a tolerance take large doses in attempts to attain the results they once achieved with regular doses. Overdose can result in unconsciousness, *coma,* and death. In addition to *physical dependence,* Amytal abuse can result in *psychological dependence. Withdrawal* symptoms can include restlessness, anxiety, insomnia, convulsions, and even death. Persons addicted to Amytal are advised not to quit *cold turkey* because of the severity of the withdrawal symptoms.

Anabolic Steroid

A type of *steroid* that mimics the male sex hormone testosterone. Anabolic steroids help build muscle and tendon strength. Medical uses include treatment of certain kinds of *anemia*, severe burns, some types of breast *cancer*, and *AIDS*. Anabolic steroids can be taken orally or by *injection*.

Anabolic steroids have more than seventy psychological and physical *side effects*. Among the most common and problematic are *jaundice* from *liver* damage, sterility, reduction of the size of the testes and breast enlargement in men, increased facial hair and decreased breast size in women, aggressive behavior, mood swings, *depression, hypertension*, permanently stunted growth in adolescents, acne, injuries to tendons and muscles, high cholesterol, and increased sexual impulses. People who inject anabolic steroids also risk contracting *HIV* from shared infected needles.

Although research is still limited, anabolic steroids are believed to cause both *physical* and *psychological dependence*. When quitting, users may experience *withdrawal* symptoms such as mood swings, fatigue, restlessness, loss of appetite, insomnia, and reduced sex drive. Drug treatment for anabolic steroid *addiction* relies primarily on counseling, since many become suicidal as the withdrawal symptoms set in. *Antidepressants* are sometimes used to treat depression, and *analgesics* are recommended for headaches and muscle pains.

Since these *drugs* stimulate the growth of muscles, they are used illegally by athletes and bodybuilders to gain an edge on the competition. Despite a ban on anabolic steroids by sports organizations throughout the world, the problem still lingers and is on the rise among adolescents.

Anabolic steroids stimulate muscle growth. They are sometimes used illegally by competitive bodybuilders.

See also:
Opioid Analgesic

Analgesic

A type of *over-the-counter* pain reliever. Most analgesics can be taken safely for seven to ten days to treat pain caused by sickness and injury.

There are three main types of analgesic. The oldest and least expensive is *aspirin*. Aspirin is a *nonsteroidal anti-inflammatory drug* (NSAID), which means that it helps to reduce swelling, among other benefits. The second type of analgesic includes *ibuprofen* and other similar drugs (ketoprofen, naproxen). Ibuprofen is also an NSAID but is thought to be gentler on the stomach than aspirin. The third type of analgesic is *acetaminophen,* found in common pain relievers and cold medicines. Acetaminophen is not an NSAID and lacks the anti-inflammatory abilities of the other two analgesics, but it is much easier on the stomach.

Doctors recommend these relatively safe over-the-counter drugs for short periods of time. Each of them can have negative effects on the body if taken in large *doses* or for an extended time.

Anemia

A condition marked by a decrease in the number of red blood cells or a depletion of hemoglobin, which is found in red blood cells. Hemoglobin is the substance that carries oxygen from the *lungs* through the bloodstream to all parts of the body. In anemia, the blood cannot carry enough oxygen to enable the organs to function properly.

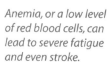

Symptoms of anemia include fatigue, weakness, lightheadedness, shortness of breath, nausea, loss of appetite, dizziness, bleeding gums, yellow eyes and skin, and confusion. When anemia is allowed to worsen, the symptoms can become dangerous, potentially resulting in *stroke* or *heart attack*.

The most common cause of anemia is excessive bleeding, but it can also be caused by decreased red blood cell production and increased red blood cell destruction. It can result from the abuse of a large number of *drugs*. Viruses, *toxins,* chemicals, and drugs prevent the body from producing a sufficient quantity of healthy red blood cells.

Anemia, or a low level of red blood cells, can lead to severe fatigue and even stroke.

Antabuse

Anesthetic

A *drug* that eliminates sensation in the body. Anesthetics are usually used during surgery and other medical procedures, but they can also be used to treat pain caused by certain illnesses and injuries. There are three main types of anesthetic: general, local, and topical.

General anesthetics eliminate sensation throughout the body and are accompanied by unconsciousness. This type is most frequently used during major surgical operations.

Local anesthetics deaden sensation in particular areas of the body by interfering with pain signals sent by nerves to the brain. *Novocaine* is a local anesthetic commonly used in dentistry. Local anesthetics can be *injected* into a specific area of the body or applied as a lotion as in the case of *benzocaine*.

Topical anesthetics are lotions or ointments applied to an area to reduce or eliminate pain. Some topical anesthetics are used to relieve the pain associated with arthritic conditions. Others are mixed with mouthwash to deaden the pain of sore throats and mouths.

Some anesthetics are associated with a history of substance abuse. Perhaps the most notorious is *cocaine,* which once was popular as a local anesthetic but is rarely used today. Some surgeons still use it because it also tightens small arteries, reducing blood flow during surgery. Much like cocaine, *opium*-based drugs were once commonly used as anesthetics, until the medical world recognized how addictive these drugs can be. *Nitrous oxide* ("laughing gas") is another anesthetic that has historically been misused, although it is still customarily used as a dental anesthetic.

Antabuse

The brand name of the *drug* disulfiram, which is prescribed in pill form for alcoholics trying to quit drinking. Antabuse hinders the metabolism of *alcohol*, resulting in a buildup of a *toxin* called acetaldehyde in the bloodstream. When a person taking Antabuse ingests alcohol (including small quantities found in *cough remedies)*, acetaldehyde levels in the blood become five to ten times higher than normal.

This development results in what is known as the disulfiram-alcohol reaction, the severity of which depends upon the amounts of Antabuse and alcohol involved. Even small amounts of these two substances can cause flushing, throbbing neck, weakness, blurred vision, headache, hyperventilation, nausea, profuse vomiting, sweating, thirst, confusion, and *cardiac arrhythmia.* Worse reactions may include *heart attack,* respiratory

See also:
Delirium Tremens

depression, *heart failure,* convulsions, and death. These effects begin approximately fifteen minutes after consuming alcohol and last from half an hour to three hours. Alcoholics should wait a week after their last drink before taking Antabuse to avoid the effects described.

The severity of these effects is designed to keep the alcoholic from drinking, regardless of *withdrawal* symptoms. Antabuse should not be considered a cure for *alcoholism* by itself; it is most beneficial when combined with counseling and other rehabilitation methods. Patients must be advised of the effects of mixing alcohol and Antabuse and should never be forced to take this drug.

It is possible to *overdose* on Antabuse. Symptoms include drowsiness, nausea, vomiting, aggressive behavior, paralysis, and *coma.* Extended use of Antabuse does not cause *tolerance.* The longer the patient takes Antabuse, however, the more sensitive he or she will become to alcohol.

Antacid

A type of *over-the-counter drug* taken to neutralize acid in the digestive system. The stomach produces hydrochloric acid to digest food. This acid can cause discomfort and pain for people who have peptic ulcers (open sores in the lining of the stomach). Antacids can relieve this pain by neutralizing the acid. People who experience indigestion and heartburn (pain caused by the rising of stomach acid into the esophagus) also commonly take antacids.

Antacids come in pill, caplet, and liquid form. Four main active ingredients are found in different types of antacid.

Sodium bicarbonate (the active ingredient in baking soda) is effective and quick. This type should be avoided by people who have *hypertension,* however, because of the high salt content.

Calcium carbonate and calcium phosphate are also effective and fast-acting but can cause constipation. Prolonged use of calcium antacids can cause *kidney* problems, particularly kidney stones.

Magnesium is a mild *laxative* and is therefore often combined with aluminum, which counteracts the laxative effect. Like calcium, magnesium can cause kidney stones. Too much magnesium can cause a dangerous drop in blood pressure and respiratory function.

Aluminum salt, which can cause constipation, is often mixed with one of the other three. Extended use of aluminum antacids can lead to osteoporosis (weak and brittle bones).

Some antacids contain the chemical simethicone, which safely breaks up gas bubbles in the digestive system.

Although antacids are not addictive, they should not be used for extended periods of time. Digestive problems that last longer than two weeks are most likely a sign of a greater problem, and consultation with a doctor is recommended.

Antianxiety Drug

See also:
Delirium Tremens

A type of *prescription drug* used to treat anxiety disorders, such as panic disorder and phobias. Typical antianxiety drugs include *benzodiazepines, hypnotic-sedatives,* and *tranquilizers.* Before these *drugs* were commonly prescribed, *barbiturates* were used to treat anxiety disorders. Barbiturates, however, have a high potential for abuse and are more likely than benzodiazepines to result in death in case of *overdose.*

Antianxiety drugs help relieve stress by relaxing muscles, reducing tension, and relieving insomnia. Negative effects include slurred speech, poor motor skills, confusion, slowed breathing, *depression,* memory loss, loss of concentration, and severe mood swings. Older people who take these drugs may experience dementia, as well as broken bones from accidents because of the inability to walk without help. An overdose can lead to unconsciousness and death.

Although antianxiety drugs aid deep sleep, they also obstruct REM (rapid eye movement) sleep, the sleep during which dreaming takes place. Disruption of dreaming can cause one to feel sleepy and irritable the next day. Conversely, people who quit using antianxiety drugs may experience more REM sleep than normal, which can cause frequent waking and disruption of healthy sleep.

Antianxiety drugs can cause both *physical* and *psychological dependence* after as little as two weeks. Most people who become addicted to antianxiety drugs began taking them for medical purposes. *Withdrawal* symptoms resemble those of *alcoholism* and can include nervousness, sleeplessness, dehydration, confusion, *seizures,* and even death. Benzodiazepine withdrawal is usually not as severe as barbiturate withdrawal, but symptoms may be experienced for up to a month. Drug treatment for antianxiety *addiction* requires close medical attention.

Antibiotic

Antibiotic

A type of *drug* used to fight bacterial infections. Antibiotics are of two main types: bactericidal antibiotics, which kill bacteria, and bacteriostatic antibiotics, which prevent bacteria from multiplying.

Antibiotics are often given by *injection* to control the infection and then continued orally. Treatment must continue for several days after the infection is gone to avoid a *relapse*. Antibiotics are sometimes taken as a preventive course of action, as when someone is exposed to meningitis (a bacterial disease that affects the brain and spinal cord).

Many kinds of antibiotic are used for bacterial infections all over the body. Some are used to treat a wide variety of infections; others are used for specific infections such as *tuberculosis*. Antibiotics can have an abundance of *side effects*, including diarrhea, nausea, vomiting, sensitivity to sunlight, headache, rash, fever, and chills.

Antibiotics (pictured in microscopic detail above) kill bacterial infection, but overuse may lessen or even eliminate their effectiveness.

More serious but rarer symptoms include *hepatitis*, a decrease in white blood cell count, and damage to the eye, the ear, the *kidney*, the brain, and the nerves. Allergic reactions to antibiotics, as with *penicillin*, are common, but sometimes the benefit outweighs the negative effects.

Because of the overuse of antibiotics in modern times, some forms of bacteria have developed that resist antibiotics. Although new and more powerful antibiotics are being developed, eventually bacteria will become resistant to them, too.

Antidepressant

A *prescription drug* designed to treat a variety of mental illnesses, particularly *depression*, anxiety disorders, and obsessive-compulsive disorder (a condition in which one is burdened by unwanted thoughts or the compulsion to repeat certain activities because of an irrational fear). Antidepressants have recently been used for other illnesses, such as bulimia, *cocaine cravings*, chronic pain, headache, and sleep disorders.

Antidepressants are believed to act by regulating the amount of neurotransmitters (chemical messengers) in the brain. After several weeks of taking an antidepressant, *receptors* in the brain work more efficiently because of the modified presence of neurotransmitters.

See also:
Ritalin

Although the medical community has recently developed newer versions of this type of *drug*, there are three main types of antidepressant: *tricyclic antidepressants, selective serotonin reuptake inhibitors,* and *monoamine oxidase inhibitors.*

Sometimes drugs known as psychostimulants are used as antidepressants. Unlike the other antidepressants, these drugs take only about a day to become effective and therefore have a high potential for abuse.

Except for a few extreme cases, *tolerance* and *addiction* to antidepressants are rare. Most problems occur when a person fails to take a large enough *dose* or abruptly stops using these prescribed drugs. At this point, *withdrawal* symptoms may occur: nausea, vomiting, cramps, diarrhea, chills, insomnia, and anxiety. These symptoms may last from three to five days. It is also possible, however, to *overdose* on antidepressants.

Antidote

A substance that defends the body from *poisons*. Antidotes act in one of three ways: (1) they may chemically attack the poison, making it harmless; (2) their action in the body may be the direct opposite of the action of the poison, counteracting its effects; (3) they may prevent body cells from reacting to the effects of the poison.

Most antidotes are effective against only one type of poison and could worsen the effects of other poisons.

An example of an antidote is the *drug* naloxone, which counteracts the effects of *morphine* and *heroin* in cases of *overdose*. Another antidote is antivenin, which is injected in cases of poisonous snakebite.

Antifungal Drug

A *drug* used to fight fungal infections on the skin or inside the openings of the body. These drugs may be applied to the skin as a cream or lotion, taken orally, or *injected.*

Fungal infections are caused by fungi spores that float in the air almost everywhere in the world. These spores land on the skin or are inhaled. Most fungal infections are relatively harmless, but some can cause severe infections, sometimes even in the *lungs* or *liver.*

Since fungal infections can go unnoticed for months or years, they can be particularly difficult to treat. Antifungal drugs are also somewhat ineffectual and can take a long time to rid the body of infection. Often the drug must be taken for weeks before progress is noticed, and even then the treatment must be repeated.

Antihistamine

Antifungal drugs have an abundance of *side effects,* including rash, chills, headache, fever, vomiting, lowering of potassium in the blood, and blockage of testosterone production. Long-term effects may include *kidney,* liver, and bone marrow damage.

People with impaired *immune systems,* such as those who have *AIDS,* are more likely to contract fungal infections. The infection sometimes moves through the body to the bones, kidneys, and *central nervous system.* Thrush (infection of the mouth) is a particularly common fungal infection in people who have impaired immune systems.

Antihistamine

A type of *drug* found in *over-the-counter* and *prescription* medications used to combat allergy symptoms, including irritated eyes, runny nose, sneezing, and hives. Antihistamines are found in allergy medications, but also in cold formulas, *sleep aids,* and *motion sickness drugs.*

Histamine is a chemical the body releases when it comes in contact with an allergen (something to which the body is allergic), such as dust or pollen, an insect bite, or a bee sting. Histamine *receptors* are triggered by the allergen, and histamine is released into the bloodstream. Histamine in turn causes an allergic reaction. Dangerous reactions may include *low blood pressure,* breathing difficulty, and swelling in the throat that can restrict breathing. Antihistamines block histamine receptors, thus negating the effects of allergens in the body.

Antihistamines have several other effects on the body. They dry up the respiratory system, including runny noses, which is why they are commonly found in cold medicines. This can be helpful to a cough caused by an allergy, but harmful in the case of a cough caused by a cold or viral infection, since antihistamines dry up respiratory fluids and make them harder to cough up.

Antihistamines are helpful in treating respiratory inflammations caused by colds and allergies.

Antihistamines also affect the *central nervous system,* causing sleepiness in most people, which is why they are often found in sleep aids. This can be dangerous, however, especially for people operating motor vehicles or other heavy machinery. New antihistamines have been developed that do not cause sleepiness. These can be obtained only with a doctor's prescription because in rare cases they have been known to cause *cardiac arrhythmia.*

Other *side effects* of antihistamines may include confusion, lightheadedness, dry mouth, constipation, difficulty in urinating, and blurred vision.

Antipsychotic Drug

A *tranquilizer* prescribed to treat mental disorders, including *mania* and manic-depressive disorder, but especially schizophrenia. These *drugs* can be used to treat dementia (decrease of mental ability and memory) in older people. In addition, antipsychotics have been used to treat the effects of certain drugs that affect the nervous system, such as *amphetamines.* Most antipsychotic drugs act by blocking the *receptors* of *dopamine* and other neurotransmitters (chemical messengers) in the *central nervous system.* Antipsychotic drugs are not a cure for mental illness; they merely relieve the symptoms. These drugs are usually taken orally or *injected.*

Antipsychotic drugs are often successful in treating mental illnesses for an extended period of time, but they may also have negative *side effects:* dry mouth, sleepiness, facial tics, blurred vision, nausea, vomiting, difficulty in urinating, muscle stiffness, weight gain, *low blood pressure,* rash, sexual dysfunction, confusion, and *depression.* More serious side effects include *seizures,* suppression of bone marrow growth, decreased white blood cells, and death. In rare cases, people develop a potentially fatal condition called neuroleptic malignant syndrome, characterized by very high fever and muscle stiffness.

An *overdose* of this type of drug may result in confusion, drowsiness, *cardiac arrhythmia,* delirium, respiratory difficulty, seizures, *blackout, coma,* and death. It is possible to develop a *tolerance* to antipsychotic drugs, but they are not believed to cause *chemical dependence.*

Currently, antipsychotic drugs are divided into two categories: typical and atypical. Typical antipsychotics are traditional drugs such as *Thorazine,* which are not used as often as they once were. Atypical antipsychotics are newer versions such as *Clozapine.*

Antiviral Drug

See also:
AZT

Antiviral Drug

A type of *drug* used to fight viral infections. Antiviral drugs disrupt infections by hindering the processes that a virus goes through to reproduce within the body. These drugs may be applied to the skin as a cream or lotion, taken orally, or *injected*.

Antiviral drugs are used to fight many types of viral infections, including influenza, respiratory infections, chicken pox, and *STDs,* particularly herpes (a term covering a variety of infections that result in painful blisters and open sores) and *HIV.*

Antiviral drugs are usually more *toxic* to human cells than *antibiotics.* In addition, viruses quickly build up a resistance to antiviral drugs.

A number of short-term *side effects* are related to antiviral drugs, including anxiousness, headache, slurred speech, pain and swelling, nausea, diarrhea, vomiting, and tremors. Long-term effects may include *seizures,* nerve damage, *kidney* damage and kidney stones, hair loss, *anemia,* and bone marrow and *liver* damage.

Aspirin

Aspirin, or acetylsalicylic acid, is an *over-the-counter drug* used to treat pain. This type of *analgesic* is also known as a *nonsteroidal anti-inflammatory drug* (NSAID) because it blocks the inflammation that naturally accompanies burns, sprains, broken bones, and muscle strains. Since it thins the blood, aspirin is often administered to people suffering *heart attack* and coronary artery disease (obstructed blood flow in the arteries because of fatty deposits). Aspirin is often recommended for children and adults suffering from rheumatoid arthritis (extreme inflammation of the joints).

Aspirin, like all NSAIDs, can cause digestive problems, including heartburn, upset stomach, and ulcers. Since aspirin prevents normal blood clotting, it is not recommended for people with *hypertension* or bleeding disorders. Aspirin should be avoided by people who have asthma, as it can intensify the symptoms. Taken in very large *doses* for extended periods of time, aspirin can cause temporary hearing loss and stomach irritation. People who take frequent doses over a short period of time run the risk of aspirin *poisoning,* which can result in nausea, increased temperature, and sometimes convulsions. Children and teenagers who have influenza or chicken pox should not take aspirin because it could lead to a rare, life-threatening disease known as Reye's syndrome (inflammation of the brain and rapid accumulation of fat in the *liver*).

AZT

An *antiviral drug* commonly prescribed to treat *HIV* infection. Some people with HIV take AZT in pill form several times a day.

AZT helps prevent HIV from reproducing, thus delaying the progression of the disease and the development of *AIDS*. AZT and other *drugs* like it are known as reverse transcriptase inhibitors. Researchers have discovered that HIV uses an enzyme called reverse transcriptase to reproduce, and drugs such as AZT interfere with this process. Research shows that pregnant women with HIV who take AZT are one-third less likely to transmit the virus to the unborn child.

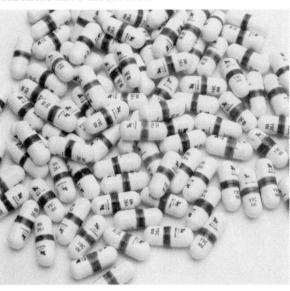

While not everyone experiences them, AZT can cause mild to severe *side effects,* including headache, nausea, vomiting, dizziness, and sometimes *seizures.* Long-term effects may include *hypertension,* loss of muscle, bone marrow damage, and *anemia.* In almost every case, HIV develops a resistance to AZT. This can happen after only a few days or after years of use. A few *overdoses* have been reported. Most often, the effects of AZT overdose are nausea and vomiting; no deaths have been reported.

AZT is thought of as the most effective drug treatment for HIV. Recent studies in Asia, however, have shown the drug to be ineffective and even harmful to some individuals. Most of these studies focus on the growing number of *birth defects* in babies born to women who take AZT. In addition, some researchers have reported that AZT can be more harmful for children than helpful.

AZT, considered the most effective drug for treating HIV, helps prevent the virus from reproducing.

B

- Barbiturate
- Benzocaine
- Benzodiazepine
- Binge Drinking
- Birth Defects
- Blackout
- Blood Alcohol Level
- Bong
- Breast-Feeding
- Breathalyzer
- Bronchitis
- Bupropion
- Butyl Nitrite

Barbiturate

Synthetic depressant often prescribed as an *antianxiety drug,* an *anesthetic,* and/or a *hypnotic-sedative.* Barbiturates are prescribed to treat anxiety disorders, insomnia, and epilepsy. Most barbiturates come in pill form, although some can be *injected* into the body, particularly those used as anesthetics.

Similar to *alcohol,* barbiturates affect the *central nervous system* and depress brain functioning. Small amounts of barbiturates produce a calmness and sleepiness, and help to relax muscles. Larger *doses* can produce slurred speech, staggering, and slowness of reflexes. Other short-term effects can include difficulty in breathing, *low blood pressure,* mood swings, violent behavior, fatigue, lack of coordination, and *depression.*

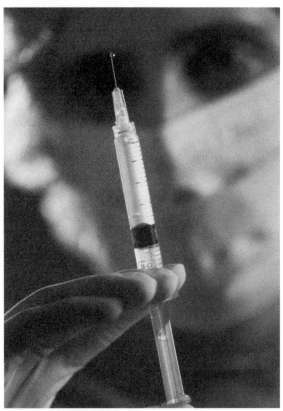

Barbiturates have a high potential for *drug abuse.* Many people become addicted to legally prescribed barbiturates, and many others take them illegally to escape depression and other anxiety disorders, or just to get *high.* Prolonged use of barbiturates can lead to *physical* and *psychological dependence.* Users can rapidly build up a *tolerance* and require larger doses to achieve the high. This situation frequently leads to *overdoses,* which can result in unconsciousness, *coma,* and death (approximately one-third of all drug-related deaths involve barbiturate overdoses). Another risk associated with barbiturate abuse is mixing them with alcohol, a deadly combination since both depress *heart* and *lung* functioning.

The *withdrawal* symptoms of barbiturate *addiction* are severe; as bad as or worse than those of *heroin* addiction. Withdrawal symptoms can include convulsions, severe paranoia, and even death. People addicted to barbiturates are advised not to quit *cold turkey* but to decrease the dosage under a doctor's supervision until the symptoms are manageable.

Barbiturates are sometimes used as anesthetics to prepare patients for surgery.

Benzocaine

A local *anesthetic* similar to *novocaine.* This *drug* is used to treat minor pain and itching, and can be found in certain *over-the-counter drugs.* Benzocaine is used to treat insect bites, sunburn, minor wounds, and hemorrhoids. As a *cough remedy,* it numbs the back of the throat, and as a *diet aid,* it numbs the taste buds. Unlike novocaine and other anesthetics, benzocaine is only applied to the skin, never *injected.*

Negative *side effects* of this drug may include allergy symptoms, such as rash, itching, hives, and swelling of the mouth and throat. These symptoms can cause a blockage of the airways, becoming potentially life-threatening. Rare side effects include drowsiness, ringing in the ears, and anxiety.

Benzocaine led to the development of novocaine in the early 1900s. Both of these anesthetics were derived from *cocaine,* which had been the anesthetic most doctors chose to use. Unlike cocaine, benzocaine is not addictive.

Benzodiazepine

Depressant frequently prescribed for insomnia and anxiety disorders. Like *barbiturates,* benzodiazepines are also used to treat epilepsy and as an *anesthetic.* They depress *central nervous system* activity and brain functioning. The *drug* is usually taken in pill form.

Benzodiazepines are considered the safest of the *hypnotic-sedatives* because they are less disruptive to deep sleep, their effects are less *euphoric* in nature, and there is somewhat less risk of death by *overdose.* As a result, they are more often prescribed for sleeplessness and anxiety than other depressants.

In small *doses,* benzodiazepines reduce stress, promote sleep, and relax muscles. In large doses, they can result in unconsciousness, *coma,* and death. Benzodiazepines remain in the system longer than other hypnotic-sedatives, and some long-lasting types can be particularly dangerous for older people.

Other negative *side effects* can include slurred speech, confusion, slowed breathing, *depression,* memory loss, and mood swings. Despite their relative safety as depressants, benzodiazepines have a high potential for substance abuse. Long-term use quickly leads to *physical* and *psychological dependence, tolerance,* and *withdrawal* symptoms similar to those of *alcoholism.* People addicted to benzodiazepines are not advised to quit *cold turkey,* since the withdrawal symptoms can lead to extreme paranoia, *seizures,* and even death. Instead, they should cut back slowly until the symptoms are manageable.

Benzodiazepines are not considered "party" drugs because they lack the euphoric effects of depressants like barbiturates. When combined with other *narcotics,* however, their effects are heightened and can become even more dangerous.

Binge Drinking

Consuming multiple alcoholic drinks one after another on at least one occasion. Some binge drinkers have taken five or more drinks in a short period of time on several occasions. Binge drinking is more injurious than drinking the same amount spread over several occasions. Drinking ten ounces of whiskey in one sitting, for example, is more harmful to your body than drinking ten ounces in one week.

Short-term effects of binge drinking include nausea, vomiting, impaired mental and physical abilities, and severe *hangover.* Binge drinking can lead to a multitude of physical, mental, emotional, and social problems: poor educational and athletic performance, absence from school or work, *depression, DWI* (driving while intoxicated)-related accidents and deaths, suicide, accidental death, injury to self and others, sexual assault, violence, vandalism, and other *crime*-related activities, and a wide variety of health risks. Binge drinking often leads to unwanted pregnancies and the transmission of *STDs* when people neglect safe-sex practices.

Most research on binge drinking focuses on college students because it has become so common in that population. Binge drinking often occurs in "party" or social situations when many young people are gathered together and in a festive mood. Happy hours, drink specials, drinking contests, youth-related *alcohol* advertising, keg parties, and fraternity/sorority initiations are some of the causes that lead to widespread college binge drinking.

See also:
Alcohol
Alcoholism
Alcohol Poisoning
Date-Rape Drug

Birth Defects

Unborn children can develop numerous birth defects when the mother uses/abuses *drugs* and *alcohol* during *pregnancy.* The fetus is highly vulnerable to birth defects when its organs are developing, from seventeen to fifty-seven days after fertilization. Drugs taken after this stage may not have an obvious effect on the newborn, but defects may still manifest themselves as the child grows in the form of learning disabilities and emotional problems. Birth defects caused by drug use range from low birth weight to malformations to miscarriage (delivery of fetus before it can live outside the womb).

See also:
Fetal Alcohol Syndrome

Women who *smoke cigarettes* commonly have babies who have low birth weight and who are smaller than average babies. Drinking alcohol during pregnancy is the primary cause of birth defects. Other drugs, particularly *cocaine* and *heroin,* have been proven to cause birth defects. Marijuana is believed by some researchers to lead to birth defects, but results are inconclusive.

It is not only illicit or social drugs, however, that lead to birth defects; anticancer drugs, sex hormones, *antibiotics,* and anticonvulsant drugs can also cause them. Some researchers think that even *caffeine* can cause birth defects.

Medical authorities recommend that women consult their doctors before taking drugs while pregnant and abstain from any substance that may endanger the life of their unborn child.

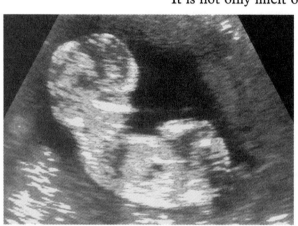

A developing fetus is highly vulnerable to birth defects, and a mother's drug and alcohol abuse frequently causes such defects.

Blackout

Also called fainting, a blackout is a temporary loss of consciousness caused by lack of oxygen reaching the brain. Blackouts are usually preceded by dizziness, weakness, or nausea.

Low blood pressure and restricted breathing are the essential causes of blackouts. They can be caused by sudden stress, pain, or fear; coughing fits; straining while trying to urinate or defecate (usually in the elderly); standing up too quickly; *diabetes mellitus; cardiac arrhythmia; heart failure; heart* diseases; *lung* diseases; *stroke;* exercise; injuries; *anemia;* and *alcohol.* Some *drugs* (especially those that are inhaled) cause blackouts because they decrease the amount of oxygen the brain receives; others (particularly *depressants*) lower blood pressure.

Since fainting is sometimes a sign of a more serious problem, people who experience frequent or occasional blackouts should see a doctor. Some may need prescribed drugs to raise blood pressure, particularly *ephedrine* and salt tablets. Others may need more serious attention.

Excessive alcohol consumption and *binge drinking* can lead to an alcoholic blackout, which is different from a regular blackout. The person may continue to interact and communicate with others but not remember his or her actions the next day. An alcoholic blackout is similar to amnesia. For this reason, alcohol is considered the most common *date-rape drug.*

Blood Alcohol Level

A measure of the amount of *alcohol* in the bloodstream. Blood alcohol level (BAL) is measured in milligrams of alcohol per deciliter of blood. Someone who has a BAL of 0.05 has 50 milligrams of alcohol per deciliter of blood.

Blood alcohol level can be measured by a *Breathalyzer* or similar device. Law enforcement officials commonly check an individual's BAL when suspecting *DWI*. The following table shows the effects of different BAL percentages on the body.

See also:
Breathalyzer

BAL %	Effects
.02–.03	Mild relaxation
.05–.06	Loss of inhibitions, exaggerated behavior, intensified emotions, mild euphoria
.08–.09	Slurred speech, loss of balance, impaired motor skills, impaired vision
.14–.17	Severe impairment of judgment and perception, aggressiveness, possible blackout
.20	Confusion, inability to stand and walk normally, nausea, vomiting, blackout, loss of memory
.25	Grave impairment of mental and physical functions, unconsciousness, asphyxiation due to vomiting
.30	Stupor, alcohol poisoning, unconsciousness
.35	Level of surgical anesthetic, breathing may stop
.40	Coma, possible death from heart failure, cardiac arrest, slowed respiration

Bong

See *Pipe*.

Breast-Feeding

Feeding a baby from a mother's breast rather than from a bottle. During breast-feeding, substances in the mother's system are passed to the child. As a result, mothers are cautioned against taking unnecessary medications.

It is acceptable to use certain *over-the-counter* and *prescription drugs* while breast-feeding, but a nursing mother should always check with her physician first. Mothers taking drugs while breast-feeding should watch out for negative *side effects* in the baby, including rash, lack of appetite, upset stomach, and poor disposition.

Drinking *alcohol* while breast-feeding can interfere with a baby's sleep and can cause lack of nourishment. Women who drink heavily while breast-feeding in the first twelve months of the baby's life risk causing the child brain damage as well as disrupting their ability to care for the baby. It is also best to avoid *smoking* altogether when breast-feeding.

The babies of breast-feeding mothers who use illicit drugs (*marijuana, cocaine, heroin, LSD,* etc.) often display restlessness, drowsiness, and poor appetite. A woman dependent on these drugs can pass the dependence to her child, who may experience *withdrawal* symptoms between feedings.

Breathalyzer

A device used to measure *blood alcohol level.* Breathalyzers and other similar devices have been used since 1962 in law enforcement, especially during *DWI* traffic stops and arrests. The device consists of an electronic component and a tube into which the subject blows. Chemicals within the unit react to alcohol in the breath sample, and BAL is computed from this reaction.

Bronchitis

Short-term or long-term inflammation of the mucous linings of the *lungs.* This causes abnormal levels of mucus to be produced by the bronchial tubes. Bronchitis can be caused by *cigarette* and *marijuana smoking,* inhaling harmful fumes and *volatile solvents,* or respiratory infection. Cigarette smoking is the main cause of chronic bronchitis—a case that persists for several months and recurs over the span of a few years. Bronchitis can eventually develop into asthma or *pneumonia.*

The main symptoms of bronchitis include a persistent cough that brings up mucus, chest pain, and fever. Acute bronchitis usually lasts for a short time. Chronic bronchitis can result in shortness of breath, respiratory failure, and possibly even *cardiac arrest.* People with chronic bronchitis sometimes develop *emphysema.*

Bronchitis may be treated with a number of *drugs* that expand the bronchial tubes to allow easier breathing and some that loosen mucus buildup, making it easier to cough up. If an infection develops, *antibiotics*

Butyl Nitrite

can be prescribed. Acute bronchitis often clears up within a few weeks. Chronic bronchitis is a permanent condition.

Bupropion

A *prescription drug* originally used as an *antidepressant* (particularly one called *Wellbutrin*). It is currently used more often to help people quit *smoking tobacco* (particularly in a product called *Zyban*). Bupropion is a *stimulant* that changes the levels and effects of certain neurotransmitters (chemical messengers) in the *central nervous system,* efficiently treating *depression.* It is not known why the drug prevents *cravings* for *nicotine.* Bupropion is taken orally and becomes effective in one to two weeks.

Besides its helpful effects, bupropion may also cause *side effects*: dry mouth, insomnia, restlessness, irritability, headache, constipation, nausea, vomiting, tremors, and weight loss. Less common side effects include *hallucinations, mania,* and *seizures.* An *overdose* of bupropion may cause blurred vision, dizziness, nausea, vomiting, sleepiness, confusion, hallucinations, and seizures; in rare cases, an overdose has led to *low blood pressure, cardiac arrhythmia, heart failure,* fever, stupor, *blackout, coma,* and death. People with a history of seizures should not take this drug. Bupropion does not lead to *chemical dependence.*

Butyl Nitrite

A yellow, flammable liquid commonly misused as an *inhalant.* Butyl nitrite can be found in a number of liquid air fresheners, and in video head cleaner. On the street, it is often called "Rush" or "Locker Room.".

Unlike most inhalants—which act as *depressants*—butyl nitrite acts as a *stimulant,* speeding up the *heart* rate. It dilates the blood vessels, allowing more blood to reach the heart and lowering blood pressure. For this reason, butyl nitrite is particularly harmful to people with heart conditions. Other effects may include flushing, increased sensual awareness, headache, dizziness, nausea, coughing, and sometimes *blackout.*

Butyl nitrite, similar to but less potent than *amyl nitrite,* is considered an aphrodisiac (sexual stimulant). It is also considered a *club drug* and is used to heighten the effects of *amphetamines* and *ecstasy.*

Butyl nitrite is a stimulant; it speeds up the heart rate and blood pressure of users.

See also:
Akyl Nitrite

Caffeine

A mild *stimulant* found in more than sixty plants. An ingredient in a wide variety of products, caffeine is considered the most popular *drug* in the world.

Caffeine speeds up the *central nervous system,* resulting in extra energy and alertness. It is sometimes prescribed for certain *heart* conditions and is found in some *over-the-counter analgesics.* Caffeine is sometimes prescribed to treat migraine headaches because it constricts the dilated blood vessels that cause migraines. It is also used to treat asthma, since it widens constricted bronchial tubes. Caffeine, however, is rarely considered a medication, but rather a social drug.

Although caffeine is believed to be relatively safe, it has a number of negative *side effects.* Consumption of caffeine can lead to mood swings, anxiety, restlessness, sleeplessness, digestive problems, and headache. Caffeine has been found to cause lack of attention and hyperactivity in children.

Product	Caffeine (milligrams)
Coffee (8 ounces)	
• Strong	135–175
• Weak	80–100
• Instant	100
• Decaf	4
Tea (5 ounces)	
• Tea bag/leaf	40
• Instant	30
Soda (12 ounces)	
• Coca-Cola	35
• Mountain Dew	52
Cocoa (8 ounces)	7
Chocolate (1 ounce)	20
Wake-up Pills (1 pill)	
• NoDoz	100
• Vivarin	200
Analgesics (1 pill)	
• Anacin	32
• Excedrin	65
Diet Pills (1 pill)	100–200

Although there is no evidence that habitual caffeine use leads to cardiovascular diseases, some individuals may experience a short-term rise in blood pressure. This effect usually lasts only a few hours and has not been found to be overly dangerous to health.

Regular use of caffeine can lead to *physical* and *psychological dependence,* and users can develop a *tolerance* for caffeine. People who consume coffee every day, for example, may eventually need to drink more for the caffeine to have the same effect. People may experience *withdrawal* symptoms including headache, fatigue, and irritability when they go without caffeine for as little as a few hours.

The table on the left illustrates the caffeine content in common beverages and drugs.

See also:
Chemotherapy

Cancer

Any of approximately one hundred diseases marked by abnormal cell growth caused by a change in the cells' genetic material. Cancer cells multiply to form tumors and take over healthy cells around them. Cancerous tumors are classed in two basic types: benign (not dangerous to health) and malignant (dangerous to health because of the potential of spreading). Once malignant cancer develops, it can metastasize, or spread rapidly, through the body. Malignant cancer can result in death despite medical care.

Cancer develops for a number of reasons. Environmental *toxins* that cause cancer are called *carcinogens* and include X rays, ultraviolet radiation from the sun, chemicals, viruses, and parasites. *Smoking* is one of the most common—and most avoidable—causes of cancer. Nearly one-third of all cancer cases are caused by *tobacco* products. Tobacco can cause cancer of the mouth, gums, tongue, esophagus, larynx, trachea, pancreas, *kidney,* bladder, and most commonly, *lungs.* Even *secondhand smoke* can cause cancer. Excessive *alcohol* consumption can lead to cancer of the mouth, throat, esophagus, *liver,* and pancreas.

In addition to radiation therapy and surgery, treatment for cancer often includes a wide variety of *drugs.* Most often, a combination of methods is employed to treat cancer.

Cancer is identified by the abnormal growth of cells, which multiply rapidly, overtaking nearby healthy cells.

Cannabis Sativa

See *Marijuana.*

Carcinogen

Any environmental *toxin* that causes *cancer* by changing the genetic material in human cells. Carcinogens include ultraviolet radiation from the sun, X rays and other radiation, chemicals, viruses, and parasites.

Carcinogens are found in many areas of life and in many forms. Some common carcinogenic substances include *tobacco* products (which contain at least forty-three carcinogens), *alcohol,* some *synthetic* sweeteners, asbestos, and fatty foods. Some common carcinogens can be avoided by not *smoking, abstaining* from alcohol, eating a high-fiber/low-fat diet, and wearing sunscreen when in the sun for extended periods of time.

Cardiac Arrest

An abrupt stop in the pumping of the *heart.* Potential causes include *heart attack,* electrocution, hypothermia (body temperature dropping below ninety-five degrees Fahrenheit), loss of blood, and *drug overdose.*

Someone who experiences cardiac arrest loses consciousness and will also stop breathing. If the heart is not restarted quickly, brain damage may result from lack of oxygen. Cardiac arrest often results in death.

CPR (cardiopulmonary resuscitation) should be administered immediately to a person suffering from cardiac arrest. If CPR does not work, other methods of restarting the heart include defibrillation (applying electric shock to the heart) and an *injection* of *adrenaline,* sometimes directly into the heart. During cardiac arrest, the blood becomes overly acidic. As a result, sodium bicarbonate (the chemical in baking soda) is often given intravenously to balance the acidity. Other drugs, such as *lidocaine,* can be administered to stabilize the heart.

Even when the heartbeat can be restored, however, a number of people who have recovered from cardiac arrest die within a year because of permanent damage to the heart and brain.

Cardiac Arrhythmia

An abnormal heartbeat caused by a disruption of electrical impulses in the *heart.* The human heart beats approximately sixty to one hundred times a minute. Heartbeat is controlled by a system of nerves in and around the heart. Cardiac arrhythmia occurs when something interferes with this electrical system, making the heart beat faster, slower, or irregularly.

The number one cause of cardiac arrhythmia is heart disease, including coronary heart disease (obstructed blood flow because of fatty deposits in the arteries that supply blood to the heart), *heart attack,* heart valve defects, and *heart failure.* It can also be caused by a malfunctioning thyroid gland, stress, and by *alcohol, caffeine,* and other *drugs.*

The two main types of cardiac arrhythmia are tachycardia (faster than normal heartbeat) and bradycardia (slower than normal heartbeat).

Arrhythmia can result in irregular heartbeat, palpitations (a fluttering or pounding heartbeat), dizziness, faintness, unconsciousness, breathing difficulty, chest pain, and heart failure.

Cardiac arrhythmia is usually a sign of a worse condition, and treatment depends on what that condition is. Sometimes no treatment is necessary. Some drugs can help relieve arrhythmia but are unpredictable; some even cause worse arrhythmia. A pacemaker can be implanted in the body to keep the heartbeat regular; this is usually done in the case of bradycardia. Sometimes electric shock is administered to halt an abnormal heart rhythm (defibrillation), but this method cannot prevent arrhythmia. Certain types of arrhythmia can be corrected with surgery, as in coronary heart disease.

Central Nervous System (effects of drugs on)

The central nervous system (CNS) is made up of the brain and spinal cord. The CNS contains billions of cells called neurons, creating a system

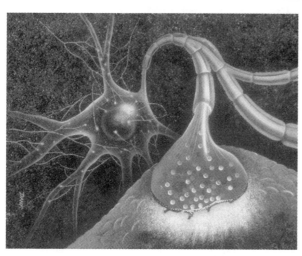

through which information is passed. Between these cells, in spaces called synapses, are chemicals called neurotransmitters, which are released by the neurons. These chemicals—such as *serotonin* and *dopamine*—help transmit messages from one nerve cell to the next. For instance, dopamine affects motor functioning, emotional responses, and feelings of pleasure and pain.

Neurotransmitters and neurons fit together like keys in locks. The neurotransmitters are "keys" that fit perfectly in specific "locks" on the neuron called *receptors*. These "keys" and "locks" form a system that conveys messages throughout the CNS. When this process is triggered in the brain by an external stimulus, an individual experiences an emotional response or a physical reaction.

The body's central nervous system, or CNS, is comprised of billions of cells called neurons (illustrated above). The CNS controls the functions of the brain and spinal cord.

Researchers believe that all addictive substances affect the way neurotransmitters work in the CNS. A *drug* can fool the brain into thinking that it is actually a neurotransmitter, causing the neurons to release higher amounts of the neurotransmitter, or blocking the neurotransmitter's effects altogether. Either reaction alters the way the brain sends, receives, and interprets messages.

When *cocaine,* for example, reaches the brain, it prevents neurons from removing dopamine from the synapses. This raises the amount of dopamine in the brain to very high levels, and the person is essentially fooled into altered feelings; this is a cocaine *high.*

Eventually, if the drug is used frequently over time, the cells of the CNS adapt to the situation and build up a *tolerance* to the presence of the drug. In addition, a sudden absence of the drug leads to *withdrawal* symptoms.

Chemical Dependence

A condition characterized by an obsession with *intoxication* by *drugs* and/or *alcohol.* People become dependent on drugs and alcohol for various reasons: to get a *high,* to escape from reality, to obtain relief from physical and mental pain, disappointment, *depression,* and anger. Chemical dependence may be *physical* or *psychological.*

Signs of chemical dependence include mood swings, depression or anxiety, frequent sickness or claims of sickness, emotional denial when confronted, listlessness, hyperactivity, inability to keep a job, recurring accidents, *binge drinking,* poor memory, and *blackouts.*

Chemical dependence can lead to a number of negative *side effects.* People who become dependent on drugs and alcohol gradually withdraw from life the more addicted they become. They may become so obsessed with the drug of choice (even though they may know its risks) that they will do anything to obtain it, including lie, manipulate friends and family members, and neglect work and school. Chemical dependence can cause physical problems—for example, *lung* disease, *heart* disease, brain damage, and *liver* disease—as well as psychological problems such as depression and anxiety. Chemical dependence can also lead to such complications as *HIV, hepatitis, overdose,* family abandonment, and death. In addition, people with a chemical dependency can develop *tolerance* to the substance and *withdrawal* symptoms when they try to stop using it.

Chemical dependency is often a sign of another problem, and physical and/or psychological treatment may be helpful in kicking the habit. Other *drug rehabilitation* methods include *intervention, detoxification,* medical care, counseling, and *twelve-step programs.*

Chemotherapy

The treatment of *cancers* or infections with *drugs* that have a *toxic* effect on the source of the sickness. Chemotherapy is often combined with surgery and radiation treatment.

Anticancer drugs act in several ways to change the DNA of cancerous cells and prevent them from replicating. Unfortunately, most of these drugs also affect healthy cells, especially rapidly dividing cells (e.g., hair), and can cause *side effects* that include nausea, vomiting, loss of appetite, hair loss, low blood cell count, deficient *immune system*, skin rash, *kidney failure*, and low sperm count.

Depending on the situation, chemotherapy can be conducted at a hospital, in a doctor's office, at home, in an outpatient location, or during surgery. Treatment schedules can also vary, from several *doses* in a day, to a single dose, to intermittent doses for weeks, months, or years. Chemotherapy can be administered by an IV drip, through *injection*, or orally.

Children may be introduced to drug use through a friend or close relative.

Children and Drugs

Children begin using *drugs* for numerous reasons, not just because of *peer pressure*. Many kids see adults drinking and *smoking* on television and in real life and think that they will be adult by doing the same. Some think it looks cool or begin doing drugs out of boredom or to satisfy their curiosity. Other are seeking relief from their troubles or a way to show their independence.

Although some kids stop using drugs after *experimenting*, others continue to use *recreational drugs,* and some develop *physical* and/or *psychological dependence*. Research has shown that kids who use cigarettes and alcohol are more likely to use marijuana; kids who use marijuana are more likely to use other addictive drugs.

Children today are influenced in many ways by drugs. Television, radio, and print advertising presents use of alcohol and cigarettes as ways to fit into fashionable society. Even *caffeine* is touted as a hip and trendy drug to consume. Children often see their parents, brothers, sisters, and other relatives using social drugs. Kids whose parents have a history of *addiction* are more likely to develop their own addiction. Drugs have become exceedingly easy for children to obtain, further perpetuating the cycle of addiction found in many families.

Parents should warn their kids about the dangers of drugs at an early age and provide healthy options to fill their time: sports, music lessons, religious functions, social gatherings, family outings, an enjoyable job, community projects, and so on. It is also important for parents to be vigilant for *signs of drug use* so they can prevent it from becoming a serious problem.

Chloral Hydrate

A *hypnotic-sedative* primarily prescribed to treat insomnia. It is also used to help patients relax before surgery or as a minor pain reliever following surgery. Chloral hydrate is one of the oldest hypnotic-sedatives, and other *drugs* (especially *benzodiazepines*) are more often used. Chloral hydrate can be taken orally or rectally.

Like all hypnotic-sedatives, chloral hydrate depresses the *central nervous system*. People who take this drug usually fall asleep within an hour. *Side effects* of chloral hydrate may include rash, nausea, stomach pain, vomiting, lightheadedness, dizziness, and diarrhea; less common side effects are confusion and *hallucinations*. *Overdose* symptoms include confusion, *seizures*, extreme fatigue, low body temperature, nausea, vomiting, *cardiac arrhythmia*, slurred speech, staggering, unconsciousness, *coma*, and death. Chloral hydrate can produce similarly negative effects when taken with other drugs such as *tranquilizers*, *alcohol*, *barbiturates*, or *anesthetics*.

Chloral hydrate can lead to *physical* and *psychological dependence*. The drug is commonly abused by people who have difficulty in sleeping, including alcoholics. Individuals can build a *tolerance* for it and eventually need to increase the *dosage* to attain the same results. When they try to stop using chloral hydrate, they may experience *withdrawal* symptoms such as confusion, hallucinations, nervousness, insomnia, stomach pain, tremors, and anxiety or excitement.

Cigarette/Cigar

Tobacco wrapped in paper or tobacco leaf for *smoking*. Cigarettes commonly have filters through which the smoke passes before it is inhaled, while cigars are primarily smoked without filters. Cigarettes have had a long history in the United States, illustrated by the time line below; they continue to be the subject of much controversy today.

History of Cigarettes in the United States

1880s Cigarettes gain popularity partly because of the first cigarette rolling machine.

1910s Cigarettes are given to United States soldiers in World War I.

1919 First cases of lung cancer are recorded.

1926 First cigarette ads aimed at women appear.

1930 Official correlation between cigarettes and cancer is discovered in Germany.

1944 American Cancer Society starts to warn of health risks associated with cigarettes.

1952 *Reader's Digest* article ("Cancer by the Carton") reveals dangers of smoking to the American public.

1953 Cigarette sales decline for the first time since before 1930.

1954 First lawsuit filed against the tobacco industry fails.

1954 The Tobacco Industry Research Council is founded; filtered cigarettes are introduced.

1964 Surgeon General Luther Terry links lung cancer to cigarette smoke.

1965 Surgeon general's warning is placed on all cigarette packages.

1967 Equal time is mandated for smoking and antismoking ads on television.

1970s Lung cancer—once one of the rarest cancers—becomes the number one form of cancer in the United States.

1971 Cigarette ads are banned from television and radio.

1985 Lung cancer becomes number one cause of cancer death in women.

1988 Tobacco industry is successfully sued by widow of a cancer victim.

1990 Smoking is prohibited in government offices.

1990 Smoking is banned on United States airline flights under six hours.

1994 Mississippi is the first of twenty-two states to sue cigarette companies for the Medicaid bills of former smokers.

1995 Legislation authorizes the FDA to regulate the sale and advertisement of tobacco products.

1995 Smoking is banned in all California restaurants.

1998 Smoking is banned in all California bars.

1998 $206 billion master settlement agreement is reached between the tobacco industry and forty-six states, giving compensation for the treatment of sick smokers and damages incurred by cigarette smoking.

2000 Philip Morris Inc. and R.J. Reynolds Tobacco Holdings Inc. raise the wholesale price of their cigarettes by fourteen cents a pack, the industry's third price increase of the year.

Cirrhosis of the Liver

A disease that causes the *liver* and sometimes the *kidneys* to harden and become permanently scarred. Cirrhosis of the liver is most often the result of *alcoholism,* but it can also be caused by the use of certain *drugs*, by exposure to certain chemicals, or by chronic *hepatitis.* Once cirrhosis is diagnosed, the development of liver scarring usually stops, but the scar tissue remains.

Cirrhosis prevents the liver from performing vital bodily functions such as producing proteins (which help the body fight infection) and removing harmful substances from the blood. Cirrhosis is often painless and difficult to detect in its early stages. In many cases, the earliest sign of liver disease is *jaundice.* People with acute cirrhosis become weak and disoriented. The scar tissue it forms restricts blood flow, causing high blood pressure in the vessels of the liver. This can result in internal bleeding, the accumulation of harmful fluids in the abdomen, and vomiting blood. The worst cases often result in death.

A small number of cases of cirrhosis of the liver can be controlled by diet and *abstinence* from alcohol, but there is no cure. Liver *transplant* is possible; but the "new" liver can develop cirrhosis if the person does not stop drinking or if the underlying cause of the disease is not addressed.

Clozapine

An *antipsychotic drug* used to treat schizophrenia and other mental illnesses. This *drug* is usually used after other antipsychotic drugs have failed. Clozapine adjusts the levels of certain neurotransmitters (chemical messengers) in the *central nervous system.* It is taken orally.

Negative *side effects* of Clozapine may include dry mouth, sweating, constipation, drooling, weight gain, clumsiness, muscle and joint pain, nausea, vomiting, anxiety, increased *heart* rate, *low blood pressure,* changes in vision, chest pain, *cardiac arrhythmia,* confusion, nightmares, difficulty in urinating, fever, sexual dysfunction, facial tics, *blackout,* and *seizures.* More serious side effects include extremely high fever, a decrease in white blood cells, and death.

An *overdose* of Clozapine may result in sleepiness, cardiac arrhythmia, low blood pressure, respiratory problems, drooling, delirium, seizures, blackout, *coma,* and death. Users can build a *tolerance* for it, but it is not believed to cause *chemical dependence.*

Club Drug

A type of *drug* commonly used at dance clubs and raves (all-night dances held in secret locations) for their resulting *euphoria*. These drugs produce varying effects—ranging from increased *heart* rate and a boost of physical energy to decreased heart rate and a sensation of detachment from reality—but are grouped together because they are used frequently by club crowds. Illicit drugs as well as prescription drugs are abused in clubs; they are outlined in the chart below.

Club Drug	Common Effects
Stimulants	
•*Methamphetamine*	Increased energy, euphoria, muscle pain, blurred vision, aggressive encounters. Users often dance all night.
•*Cocaine*	Increased energy, euphoria. Not popular as a club drug because it does not last as long as methamphetamine.
Hallucinogens	
•*LSD*	Increased energy; intensified lights, colors, and sounds; hallucinations; euphoria. Can lead to "bad trips."
•*MDMA (Ecstasy)*	Intensified lights, colors, and sounds; hallucinations; euphoria; increased desire to touch and dance with others.
Hypnotic-Sedatives	
•*GHB*	Relaxation, sedation, intoxication, unconsciousness, amnesia. Date-rape drug.
•*Rohypnol*	Relaxation, sedation, unconsciousness, amnesia. Date-rape drug.
•*Ketamine*	Anesthesia, sedation, floating feeling, apathy, hallucinations, unconsciousness. Date-rape drug.
Others	
•*Alcohol*	Relaxation, loss of inhibitions, intoxication, sedation, unconsciousness. Date-rape drug.
•*Viagra*	Sexual stamina, increased energy. May lead to sexual aggression.

All of these drugs can lead to *physical* and *psychological dependence* and *withdrawal* symptoms. Most can lead to death from *overdose* or mixing too many together.

Cocaine

A strong *stimulant* made from the leaves of the South American coca plant. Cocaine is a powder that is most often *snorted* but can also be taken orally, *injected,* or *freebased.* Affecting the *central nervous system,* cocaine generates a sense of profound alertness in its users, accompanied by intense feelings of well-being and power.

Cocaine was long used as a local *anesthetic* in the United States and was even marketed as a "health drink" by Coca-Cola in 1885. Today it is an illegal *drug* used primarily in a social setting; *addiction,* however, causes some people to use it many times a day, even when they are at work or alone.

Short-term effects include increased *heart* rate and blood pressure, nervousness, *hallucinations,* sleeplessness, decreased appetite, and violent behavior. Cocaine can also cause a "crawling" sensation beneath the skin, a sign of nerve damage. The initial effects wear off in twenty to forty minutes. Cocaine is highly addictive; after the *high* has worn off, users often take more to avoid the *depression* (called a *crash*) that commonly sets in.

Long-term effects include *heart attack* (often fatal), intestinal damage, nerve damage, and *seizures.* Frequent users can develop extreme cases of depression and psychosis. These symptoms can continue for months, even though use of the drug has been discontinued.

Cocaine is a highly addictive stimulant with a long history of abuse.

Frequent cocaine users develop a *tolerance* for the drug, resulting in *withdrawal* symptoms (depression, fatigue). Treatment for cocaine addiction includes counseling and psychotherapy in a residential drug-treatment facility or hospital. Some psychological disorders related to cocaine addiction (depression, suicidal tendencies) are treated with *antidepressants.*

Codeine

An *opioid analgesic* that is often prescribed as a painkiller and cough suppressant. Codeine is derived from *opium*, but it is also *synthetically* manufactured from a similar *drug, morphine,* which is derived from the poppy plant. It can be taken orally or *injected.*

Like all opiates, codeine eases (moderate) pain and creates a sense of well-being; opiates like morphine act in the same way but are much stronger than codeine. Codeine is contained in some *over-the-counter* cold medications and is commonly combined with other drugs, especially *acetaminophen.*

Codeine can cause the following *side effects:* sleepiness, dry mouth, dizziness, constipation, rashes, *depression,* blurred vision, nausea, and vomiting. Less common side effects include *hallucinations, cardiac arrhythmia,* numbness, and *seizures.* It is possible to *overdose* on codeine, which may produce nausea, vomiting, lethargy, dizziness, seizures, confusion, *coma,* and death.

Long-term use of codeine can lead to *liver* and *kidney* damage (especially when combined with acetaminophen) and stomach bleeding (especially when combined with *aspirin*). Although it has the lowest potential of the opiates for *psychological* and *physical dependence,* long-term use can build *tolerance.* Codeine *withdrawal* symptoms are similar to, but not nearly as severe as, those of *heroin addiction;* they may include muscle cramps, runny nose, aches, weakness, restlessness, and diarrhea. The symptoms generally last for two to four days, but the person may feel generally unwell for a longer time.

Codependence

A compulsive desire to please others. A codependent is often obsessed with taking care of another person, ignoring his or her own physical and emotional needs.

Codependence is a complicated disorder that may develop from a number of familial and/or social difficulties. Codependents learn to cope with emotional pain and stress by giving in to, catering to, and making excuses for specific individuals with their own problems. Even when a relationship becomes extremely unhealthy—because of *drug* use, violence, mental abuse, and so on—the codependent refuses to seek help, thinking he or she is doing what is best for the loved one. This condition can be described as a *compulsive behavior* because the person feels compelled to put the needs of others ahead of his or her own.

Codeine

See also:
Opiate/Opium

A person who continually allows another to avoid responsibility and even helps him or her in indirect ways is called an enabler. An enabler allows a friend or family member to continue destructive behavior, rather than getting the help that is needed. Drugs and *alcohol* are often deeply involved in codependent relationships.

Cold Turkey

Abruptly halting a habitual activity, particularly an *addiction* to *drugs* or *alcohol*. This is a recommended method of quitting some drugs, particularly *nicotine*. With other drugs, however, users are not advised to go cold turkey because of the severe *withdrawal* symptoms that occur, as with *barbiturates*.

The term "cold turkey" arose from the condition of the skin of an addict who quits abruptly—cold, clammy, and with goosebumps, as a result of blood moving to the internal organs and away from the skin.

Coma

A state of unconsciousness characterized by lack of responsiveness to bodily needs (such as a full bladder) and external forces (like a pinch or shout from another person). A person in a coma may exhibit some signs of life, such as breathing, blinking, and yawning. In mild forms of coma, the individual may even respond to stimulus by mumbling a few words or moving slightly.

A coma is the result of an injury or disturbance to the area of the brain that controls consciousness, particularly the inner brain stem. A disruption of this area of the brain can cause various levels of confusion and unresponsiveness, from stupor to coma. This disruption can result from a head injury, reduced blood flow to the brain, *stroke*, and *seizure*. Coma can also be caused by *poisonous* substances in the body, including those caused by advanced *kidney* and *liver* disease and by *diabetes*. *Drug overdose* and excessive *alcohol* consumption can cause coma, since drugs and alcohol are essentially *toxins*.

A person may remain in a coma for days, weeks, even years, or may never regain consciousness. In the worst case, brain death, the brain stops functioning altogether, and the patient can be kept alive only by the use of a respirator and drugs.

Some patients wake up having lost the ability to communicate but are aware of what is going on around them. Some regain consciousness but are mentally and physically impaired. Others come out of a coma with few or no complications.

Compulsive Behavior

Any action or process an individual feels compelled to continue regardless of circumstances. *Codependents* are said to exhibit compulsive behavior by remaining devoted to people who are harmful to them.

Drug and *alcohol* abuse can also be the focus of compulsive behavior. People who become *psychologically dependent* on a drug feel an overpowering desire to continue using it, despite the negative consequences. Although the drug may not be physically addictive, the user may still feel the need for it in order to function.

Cough Remedy

Over-the-counter drug, often in liquid or syrup form, used to treat coughs caused by colds.

There are two main types of cough remedies. Expectorants cause the *lungs* to produce a watery secretion, making the cough more "productive," meaning that more phlegm is brought up out of the lungs with each cough. Suppressants help to stop dry coughs by affecting the part of the brain that controls the coughing reflex.

Suppressants may contain either *antihistamines* or *codeine,* both of which can cause drowsiness. A *narcotic,* codeine is potentially addictive, and a cough remedy containing it should not be used for an extended period of time. Codeine-based cough suppressants can also cause dizziness, nausea, vomiting, constipation, and light-

Cough remedies are typically expectorants, which facilitate coughing; or suppressants, which work to control the coughing reflex.

headedness. Cough remedies that contain codeine are sometimes used as a substitute by *heroin* addicts because codeine has similar effects if enough is ingested. Both antihistamines and codeine can have negative effects when mixed with other drugs, especially *alcohol, tranquilizers,* and other *central nervous system depressants.*

Sometimes expectorants and suppressants are found in the same medicine, which may seem pointless since the suppressant cancels the ability of the expectorant to clear the lungs of fluid. It is best to use an expectorant for chest congestion and a suppressant for a dry cough.

Crack

Crack was invented by *dealers* as a safer form of *freebase cocaine*—one that is less flammable than those mixed with *ether* and *volatile solvents.* Crack is made by mixing cocaine and sodium bicarbonate (the active ingredient in baking soda) with water and then boiling the mixture until a white paste is left. This paste is dried and broken into "rocks," which are placed in a *pipe* and *smoked.*

The effects of crack are essentially the same as cocaine, except they begin sooner (eight to ten seconds), are more intense, and do not last nearly as long (fifteen minutes). Acting as a *stimulant* on the *central nervous system,* crack creates extreme *euphoria* that is highly addictive. When a crack *high* wears off, however, users experience a *crash*—profound anxiety, *depression,* fatigue, and paranoia.

Crack is more dangerous than cocaine for a number of reasons. Cheaper than cocaine, crack is much easier for young people to find and purchase. Users try desperately to avoid the crash by using more of the drug, leading quickly to *addiction;* in fact, it is believed to be the most addictive drug on earth. Some users smoke crack nonstop for several days, smoking as much as fifty rocks. At $5 to $20 a rock, this can lead to financial ruin, in addition to *physical* and *psychological dependence,* health risks, law-breaking, and social consequences.

"Crack Baby"

A term coined in the 1980s to describe an infant born to a mother who smoked *crack cocaine* during *pregnancy.* Some researchers have estimated that nearly 160,000 babies are born addicted to crack in the United States every year.

It was originally thought that babies born addicted to crack frequently had *heart* and *lung* defects and a variety of mental problems. The research, however, neglected to take into consideration that most tested mothers had abused a variety of *drugs*—not just crack or cocaine—and had contracted *STDs* before or during pregnancy. Other researchers contend that there is no direct link between cocaine and crack use and *birth defects.*

New studies show that babies born to mothers who used cocaine and crack during pregnancy twitch and tremble and are less content than other newborns. "Crack babies" are said to display states of agitation, lethargy, and extreme excitability to certain stimuli such as loud sounds and sudden movements. They also tend to be more tense than healthy babies, are weaker, and may develop learning disabilities. It should be mentioned,

however, that the mothers involved in these tests used more than just cocaine or crack during pregnancy.

Crash

Some *drugs* (*cocaine* and *crack,* for example) create intense sensations of pleasure and well-being in the user, called *euphoria.* As the drug leaves the body and these feelings wear off, users often experience the abrupt onset of powerfully negative feelings and physical *side effects,* from *depression* and anger, to nausea and headaches. This abrupt drop from an intense *high* to an equally intense low is called a crash.

This situation is the main factor in many drug *addictions.* Users enjoy the high—and dislike the crash—so much that they sometimes take enough of the drug to remain on an extended high. Gradually their bodies build a *tolerance* for it, and it becomes even harder to achieve a satisfying high. This situation results in *physical* and *psychological dependence, overdose,* and *withdrawal* symptoms, in addition to other long-term health risks.

Craving

A strong yearning for something. In *drug abuse,* cravings are an indication of *psychological* and *physical dependence.* After using a *drug* for an extended period of time, users feel an overpowering hunger for it. The body, having grown accustomed to the presence of the drug, may not function properly when the drug is absent. As a result, users may experience a variety of negative physical sensations, including hunger, nausea, headache, and fatigue. Users may also experience anger, irritability, and *depression.* These are the physical and psychological characteristics of *withdrawal* and can lead to powerful cravings for the drug. These cravings persist until the user gets more of the drug or until the body once again accustoms itself to its absence.

Cravings make *recovery* very difficult for people who are addicted to drugs or *alcohol.* Various *drug rehabilitation* methods, including *detoxification,* counseling, therapy, and *twelve-step programs,* can help to manage cravings.

Crime (related to drug use)

Crime

Crime is related to *drug* use in many ways. Certain drugs—such as *marijuana, cocaine, amphetamines, heroin,* and *LSD*—are illegal to produce or cultivate, transport, sell, or *possess*. The social drugs *tobacco* and *alcohol* cannot be purchased by those who are underage (cigarettes cannot be bought by those under eighteen; the legal drinking age is twenty-one). People who misuse and/or illegally sell *prescription drugs*—*barbiturates, opioid analgesics,* and *nitrous oxide*—are subject to criminal prosecution. Athletes sometimes face drug charges for abusing performance-enhancing drugs such as *anabolic steroids. Drug trafficking* and *dealing* are also illegal activities and generate other, primarily violent crimes. In addition, people who do not possess or use drugs, but associate with others who do, may be subject to the same punishment as users.

Simply using drugs makes a person more likely to commit crimes. Drug abusers can become self-centered, especially when they are desperate for drugs to feed their *cravings.* Some people commit crimes in trying to raise money to buy drugs. These crimes include fighting, robbery, gang activity, assault, and homicide. Statistics show that users of certain drugs— such as *methamphetamine,* alcohol, and *PCP*—are the most likely to be involved in violent activities.

Alcohol, a legal social drug, has a long list of criminal consequences. Domestic abuse, sexual abuse, gang fighting, and other crimes are precipitated by alcohol. *DWI* is an alcohol-related crime, causing property damage, personal injuries, and deaths.

Drug convictions often go hand in hand with other crimes: weapons possession, sexual assault, homicide, parole violation, property damage, and prostitution, to name just a few.

See also:
Date-Rape Drug

Cross-Drug Addiction

A broad term referring to *addiction* to multiple *drugs*. Cross-drug addiction can be divided into three categories: triggers, substitution, and concurrent use.

Triggers are drugs that provoke users to begin using a second drug. Research has shown, for example, that drinking *alcohol* can trigger a desire to *smoke cigarettes*.

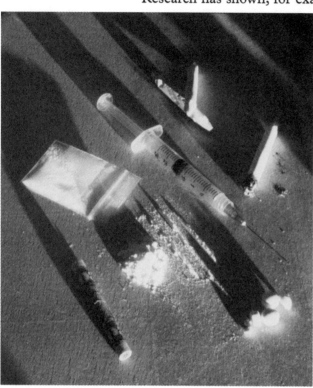

Substitution refers to switching addictions. This can happen when someone quits a certain substance and then desires a new substance to fulfill the function of the first. For instance, people who quit smoking have been known to eat more. Likewise, people addicted to *diet pills* may become obsessed with losing weight by not eating or eating very little (anorexia).

Concurrent use means that a person is addicted to two or more substances at the same time. Studies show, for example, that alcoholics under thirty are usually addicted to at least one other substance or behavior.

Cross-drug addiction is often the result of an *addictive personality* and a sign of a greater problem. Psychological counseling or *twelve-step programs* may help people regain a normal, healthy life.

Cross-drug addiction is an addiction to more than one substance.

D

- Darvon
- Date-Rape Drug
- DEA
- Dealing/Dealer
- Decongestant
- Decriminal-ization
- Delirium Tremens
- Demerol
- Depressant
- Depression
- Designer Drug
- Detoxification
- Dexedrine
- Diabetes Insipidus
- Diabetes Mellitus
- Diet Aid
- Dilaudid
- Distilled Alcohol
- DMT
- Dopamine
- Dose
- Drug
- Drug Abuse
- Drug Interaction
- Drug Rehabilitation
- Drug Testing
- Drug Trafficking
- DWI

Darvon

Darvon

The brand name for the *synthetic opioid analgesic* propoxyphene, which is most often combined with *aspirin* and/or *caffeine*. Darvon is prescribed to relieve moderate to severe pain. Similar to *methadone* but less effective, it is also sometimes used to help manage the *withdrawal* symptoms common to the use of *morphine, heroin,* and other *narcotics*. Darvon comes in pill or capsule form, and its effects last from three to four hours.

Like most narcotics, Darvon acts as a *depressant* on the *central nervous system*. In addition to reducing pain, Darvon can cause constipation, nausea, vomiting, dry mouth, decreased appetite, dizziness, fatigue, muscle spasms, and sweating. More severe *side effects* may include breathing difficulty, allergic reactions, *seizure*, and unconsciousness. An *overdose* can cause slow breathing, confusion, fatigue, cold and clammy skin, dizziness, seizures, *cardiac arrhythmia, low blood pressure, liver* damage, convulsions, unconsciousness, *coma,* and death. Darvon should not be mixed with other central nervous system depressants (especially *alcohol, barbiturates,* and other narcotics).

Commonly used to ease the pain of injury, Darvon can quickly lead to *physical* and *psychological dependence*. Users can develop a *tolerance* for it after only a week. Withdrawal symptoms related to Darvon *addiction* are similar to, but not nearly as severe as, those of heroin addiction. Most medical professionals recommend cutting down slowly rather than quitting *cold turkey,* to avoid the withdrawal symptoms.

Date-Rape Drug

A *drug* used to incapacitate a person with the intent of sexual assault. Many drugs are called date-rape drugs simply because they reduce awareness and weaken personal judgment. *Alcohol* and *barbiturates* are the most commonly used date-rape drugs.

Certain drugs, however, are notorious in date-rape, primarily *synthetic* drugs with powerful *side effects*. Rohypnol—known as *the* date-rape drug—is illegal in the United States but is a *prescription drug* in eighty other countries. Rohypnol is ten times stronger than *Valium*. *Ketamine,* an *anesthetic,* creates a floating sensation in the user and disassociation in personal behavior. Ketamine can also cause *hallucinations* and is used frequently as a *club drug*. So is *GHB,* an effective *hypnotic-sedative*.

All of these drugs can cause loss of inhibitions, confusion, drowsiness, memory loss, difficulty in speaking or moving, nausea, and *blackout*. Rohypnol and GHB are known to cause amnesia. All these drugs are highly

addictive and can result in *withdrawal* symptoms if taken over time. More serious side effects include *seizure,* halted respiration, *coma,* and death. These drugs are even more dangerous when combined with alcohol (date-rape drugs are often slipped into an individual's drink).

In 1996, the Drug-Induced Rape Prevention and Punishment Act was passed, making it a federal offense to drug a person with the intent of sexual assault. Conviction can bring a prison sentence up to twenty years. Mere *possession* of Rohypnol is punishable by up to three years in jail.

DEA

The Drug Enforcement Administration (established in 1973 under the U.S. Department of Justice) is a division of the federal government whose purpose is to enforce the *drug* laws of the United States. Its officials conduct investigations and arrests of individuals and organizations involved in growing, manufacturing, and *dealing* illegal substances for profit within and outside the United States.

The Drug Enforcement Administration, or DEA, enforces the drug laws of the United States.

The DEA works with local, state, and federal law enforcement agencies to accomplish a number of goals: investigate and prosecute persons and organizations that violate controlled-substances laws in the United States; investigate and prosecute criminals and drug gangs responsible for illegal activities related to *drug trafficking* (including violent tactics like intimidation); help local, state, federal, and foreign governments to reduce the availability of drugs; and analyze drug statistics in order to develop effective drug legislation.

The DEA works under and upholds the guidelines of the Controlled Substances Act of 1970. This act includes a number of laws governing the manufacture and distribution of controlled substances such as *anabolic steroids, depressants, hallucinogens, narcotics,* and *stimulants.*

Dealing/Dealer

The act of selling illegal *drugs,* and the person who sells them. To the law, merely giving illegal drugs to another person is considered dealing. Depending on the drug, dealing is punishable with fines and jail time more severe than for simple *possession.* Law enforcement officers are trained to

Decongestant

See also:
Crime
Drug Trafficking

watch for *signs of drug use* and also signs of dealing. These signs include having large quantities of the drug—but in small, saleable portions—and having a suspiciously large quantity of money, often in small denominations.

People from all walks of life, from wealthy businessmen to children in elementary schools, deal drugs. Some dealers work for other people in a long chain of command. For example, dealers who own the drugs they sell often make the most money from drug transactions—approximately 50 percent—if they have dealers working for them. Other dealers simply carry and/or sell drugs at a local level, making as little as 3 percent of the total profit. In between these extremes are dealers of different ranks.

Drug dealing has been estimated to generate over $100 billion a year in the United States; drug dealers from other countries also make a huge profit on U.S. drug sales. Drug dealing has also led to numerous gang-related problems, as gangs battle for selling territory and drug profits. Drug dealers and gangs sometimes employ children (ten years old and younger) to sell drugs because the punishment for youthful offenders is much more lenient than for adults.

Drug dealers come from all walks of life and may be young or old, wealthy or poor.

See also:
Diet Aid

Decongestant

Over-the-counter or *prescription drug* taken to alleviate nasal congestion from colds and allergies. Decongestants constrict the blood vessels in the nasal membranes, which reduces swelling and the amount of mucus produced by the nasal lining. The active ingredients in decongestants include *ephedrine,* pseudoephedrine, and phenylpropanolamine. Decongestants are sold as pills and drops.

Decongestants can have a number of negative *side effects,* including nervousness, *cardiac arrhythmia,* and insomnia. Decongestant drops, or sprays, can rapidly cause *physical dependence* and should be discontinued after three days. With continued use, the effects of the *drug* may become inadequate to fight congestion. This may lead to use of the drug for weeks or months. A doctor should be consulted for treatment of chronic congestion and/or allergies.

Decriminalization

Term for a movement advocating removal of felony status for *possession* of certain *drugs*, substituting at most a misdemeanor citation and/or a minimal fine. Decriminalization would uphold felony status for *dealers* who grow, manufacture, and sell drugs and participate in *drug trafficking*. One of the ideas behind this movement is that the United States is spending too much time and money on a battle that cannot be won—the "war against drugs."

For example, decriminalization is a large issue in the debate on the worthwhile uses of *marijuana*. Proponents of marijuana decriminalization maintain that in relation to drugs such as *heroin* and *cocaine*, marijuana is not only safe but holds great potential as a *prescription drug*. Those against the decriminalization of marijuana, however, believe that it may lead to a rise in criminal activity, substance *addiction*, and the decriminalization of more harmful drugs.

Currently, eleven states have decriminalization laws: Alaska, California, Colorado, Maine, Minnesota, Mississippi, Nebraska, New York, North Carolina, Ohio, and Oregon.

Delirium Tremens

The severe *withdrawal* symptoms alcoholics commonly experience when they quit drinking (similar symptoms develop in people who quit using *barbiturates*). Occurring between two and ten days after a person stops drinking, delirium tremens (or DTs) manifests as anxiety, confusion, sleeplessness, tremors, and *depression*. As it worsens, the person can experience *cardiac arrhythmia*, fever, sweating, *hallucinations*, uncontrollable shaking, convulsions, and severe panic attacks. This condition can last from three to ten days. In rare cases in which a patient has a preexisting medical condition, delirium tremens can result in death from the development of *pneumonia* or from *heart failure*.

Delirium tremens is usually treated with rest and rehydration because of fluid loss. The patient should receive close medical supervision and *injections* of *antianxiety drugs*, *acetaminophen*, and vitamins A and B.

Demerol

The brand name for the *synthetic opioid analgesic* meperidine. Demerol is similar to but not as strong as *morphine,* and it is commonly used to treat moderate to severe pain. On occasion, it is used to deaden the pain of childbirth; however, it can make the baby sluggish and hinder its breathing. Demerol can be given as a pill, syrup, or *injection.* Its effects last three to four hours. When injected, Demerol can be a very effective analgesic; orally, Demerol is less effective and may cause confusion.

As a *central nervous system depressant,* Demerol causes sedation, light-headedness, *euphoria,* and anesthesia. Negative *side effects* include dizziness, nausea, vomiting, confusion, dry mouth, headache, rash, constipation, and sweating. When injected, Demerol can cause swelling at the site. If taken too quickly or in frequent *doses,* it can result in mood swings, tremors, and *seizures.* Less common but more severe side effects are disorientation, fainting, *cardiac arrhythmia, hallucinations, low blood pressure,* convulsions, troubled breathing, and muscle spasms. An *overdose* of Demerol can result in cold, clammy, bluish skin; extreme sleepiness; cardiac arrhythmia; breathing difficulty; *heart attack; coma;* and death.

Demerol can quickly cause *physical* and *psychological dependence.* People using this drug can develop *tolerance* after only a week. *Withdrawal* symptoms are similar to those of morphine *addiction.* Most medical professionals advise addicts to cut down slowly rather than quit *cold turkey,* to avoid the withdrawal symptoms.

Demerol is frequently used as a basis for more dangerous *designer drugs.* These drugs are often referred to as "new *heroin*" because the effects are similar to those of heroin but more deadly. Demerol designer drugs have been known to cause brain damage and other physical problems.

Depressant

See also:
Delirium Tremens

Any *drug* that slows the functioning of the *central nervous system.* Depressants include *alcohol, narcotics, barbiturates, benzodiazepines, hypnotic-sedatives,* and *inhalants.* Barbiturates, benzodiazepines, and hypnotic-sedatives are prescribed to treat anxiety disorders and as *sleep aids.* Narcotics are prescribed to relieve pain and sometimes to treat certain *withdrawal* symptoms.

In addition to slowing the central nervous system, depressants also slow *heart* rate and respiration. Users often feel very relaxed, sometimes even *high.* Other *side effects* of depressants include slurred speech, loss of inhibitions, blurred vision, slowed movements, mood swings, fatigue, *depression,* and

paranoia. An *overdose* of depressants or use of two or more depressants at the same time can lead to unconsciousness, *coma,* and death.

Depressants can cause *physical* and *psychological dependence.* As the user builds a *tolerance,* larger *doses* may be required to achieve the desired effect. This often leads to overdose. Depressant withdrawal symptoms can be extremely difficult to handle and may include insomnia, anxiety, tremors, *hallucinations,* convulsions, and possibly death. People addicted to depressants often keep using them to avoid the withdrawal symptoms. *Drug rehabilitation* for depressant *addiction* may include *detoxification,* counseling, and *twelve-step programs.*

Depressants are often prescribed, but they are also widely used in social settings.

Depression

Intense feelings of sadness, negativity, and despair. Depression can originate when a person experiences a tragic or sad event—for instance, a death in the family—but it can start with no apparent reason or last for an inappropriate time (from six months to a year). Furthermore, the episodes can recur several times. Depression of this kind can be a sign of a deeper psychological problem.

Many situations and illnesses can cause depression, and it is often difficult to isolate the exact cause. Some causes include hormonal imbalances, physical illnesses and injuries, heredity, psychological illnesses, tragic events, social misfortune, and familial troubles. In addition, certain *prescription* and illegal *drugs* can cause depression, as can *withdrawal* from certain drugs. Often depression is a result of a combination of these causes.

Symptoms of depression vary depending on its severity, but all cases have some symptoms in common. The depressed person is usually irritable and/or anxious, withdrawn or shy, and experiences mood swings. Other symptoms include crying fits, loss of interest in social activities and friends, difficulty feeling emotions other than sadness and guilt, indecisiveness, difficulty falling/staying asleep, poor appetite, extreme weight loss/gain, pessimism, and slowed actions and thinking. More severe symptoms may include suicidal tendencies, visions of death, *hallucinations,* delusions, and withdrawal from life (hiding away).

See also:
Antidepressant

Treatment for depression may include hospitalization, but it is not always necessary. The two main types of treatment are psychotherapy and drug treatment. Electroconvulsive therapy (an electric shock that induces brain *seizures* to fight depression) is sometimes used in conjunction with other treatment.

See also:
Demerol

Designer Drugs

Modified versions of illegal *drugs* made in underground laboratories with the intent to create drugs not specifically listed as controlled substances by the *DEA*. Designer drugs are manufactured by changing the molecular structure of an original drug, creating a new substance, or analog.

Designer drugs are either *stimulants* or *depressants* and can be ingested in pill form, *snorted* as a powder, *smoked* in a *pipe,* or *injected.* They are more potent—and dangerous—than the drugs they are designed to mimic. These drugs, often classed as *club drugs,* are designed to make the user feel *euphoric,* energetic, and/or carefree.

The best known analogs are those derived from *fentanyl,* a *synthetic opioid analgesic* originally used as an *anesthetic.* The first fentanyl analog was alpha-methylfentanyland, or China White. It is extremely dangerous, and many *overdoses* result from injecting it.

Other common types of designer drugs are meperidine analogs. These analogs are often called "new *heroin*" and are known to cause brain damage. Still others are *methamphetamine* analogs such as *MDMA* (perhaps the most popular designer drug) and *PCP* analogs.

Side effects of designer drugs vary, but they may include sleeplessness, dry mouth, muscle tension, clenched teeth, drooling, chills, sweating, *hallucinations, depression,* paranoia, violent tendencies, irritability, anxiety, emotional sensitivity, sense of weightlessness, confusion, blurred vision, nausea, dizziness, increased *heart* rate, increased itching, impaired speech, paralysis, tremors, permanent brain damage, and death.

Designer drugs can cause *physical* and *psychological dependence,* as well as severe *withdrawal* symptoms. Perhaps more dangerous, however, is the risk of drug *poisoning.*

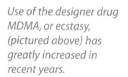

Use of the designer drug MDMA, or ecstasy, (pictured above) has greatly increased in recent years.

Detoxification

See also:
Drug Rehabilitation

The process of freeing someone from a *physical dependence* on an addictive substance. Detoxification may involve a variety of treatments, such as medical treatment, psychological testing, and counseling. Medical detoxification is only the first step in an effective drug-treatment program, as it does little by itself to curb long-term drug use. Detoxification applies primarily to the process of helping individuals through the acute physical *cravings* they may suffer when they first stop using *drugs* and/or *alcohol*.

To avoid intense *withdrawal* symptoms, some detoxification programs gradually decrease the daily *dosage* of the drug over a period of weeks. For example, in some cases of *heroin addiction*, individuals are prescribed the drugs *methadone* or *laam* to gradually curb their cravings for heroin.

Dexedrine

The brand name of the *amphetamine* dextroamphetamine, used to treat narcolepsy (sudden daytime sleep) and attention deficit hyperactivity disorder (ADHD). It is also used as a *diet aid* and occasionally to treat *depression*. The *drug* comes in pill or syrup form.

Like other amphetamines, Dexedrine is a *central nervous system stimulant* and causes increased energy and sometimes *euphoria*. Negative *side effects* include nausea, diarrhea, loss of appetite, weight loss, headache, rapid heartbeat and respiration, high blood pressure, sweating, restlessness, irritability, and aggressive behavior. Larger *doses* can result in *cardiac arrhythmia,* tremors, paranoia, *hallucinations,* violent behavior, and death from *heart failure,* excessive fever, or burst blood vessels in the brain. An *overdose* may result in confusion, convulsions, cramps, hallucinations, cardiac arrhythmia, vomiting, tremors, unconsciousness, *coma,* and death. Long-term effects can include malnutrition, *hypertension,* schizophrenia, blood vessel damage, *kidney* damage, *lung* problems, and *stroke*.

Extended use of Dexedrine can lead to *physical* and *psychological dependence. Tolerance* can develop quickly. When trying to quit Dexedrine, addicts usually experience moderately severe *withdrawal* symptoms, including intense hunger, irritability, long but disrupted sleep, depression, violence, and paranoia. *Drug rehabilitation* may include *detoxification,* counseling, and *twelve-step programs.*

In rare cases, people can take Dexedrine as a medication for many years; others cannot take it for long because of adverse reactions. Like other amphetamines, however, Dexedrine has a history of being abused. Some people crush the pills into powder and *snort* it for a quick, intense *high* similar to *cocaine*. Others abuse it as a diet aid.

Diabetes Insipidus

A disease characterized by the inability of the *kidneys* to retain sufficient levels of water in the body, resulting in excessive urination. People with diabetes insipidus lack the hormone vasopressin, which naturally holds water in the system. Without it, the kidneys excrete large amounts of urine, resulting in dehydration and thirst, and in worse cases *low blood pressure*, confusion, and *coma.*

Diabetes insipidus may be caused by inactivity of the hypothalamus gland, which produces vasopressin, or by failure of the pituitary gland to release that hormone into the bloodstream. *Drug* use, injury to the brain, and brain tumor can also cause the disease.

Treatment most often entails using a *synthetic* form of vasopressin, usually in nasal spray form. Other drugs stimulate the production of vasopressin in the pituitary gland. Of the two forms of diabetes, diabetes insipidus is the more rare.

Diabetes Mellitus

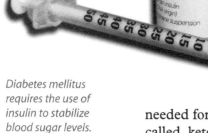

A disease characterized by excessive sugar in the bloodstream. *Insulin,* produced by the pancreas, helps cells to use sugar to create energy. People with diabetes mellitus either lack insulin and have difficulty metabolizing sugar, which builds up in the blood, or they have too much insulin, which causes the body to develop resistance to its effects, simulating an insulin deficiency.

With higher-than-normal levels of sugar in the bloodstream (hyperglycemia), the *kidneys* excrete more water to flush it from the body, causing excessive urination. The person may feel thirsty from the loss of water and hungry from the loss of calories. Other symptoms include blurred vision, fatigue, nausea, and lack of energy. Without the sugar

Diabetes mellitus requires the use of insulin to stabilize blood sugar levels.

needed for energy, the body begins to burn fat cells, which produces toxins called ketones. If the symptoms continue, the person can lapse into a diabetic *coma.*

Diabetes mellitus must be treated to keep blood sugar at a safe level in order to prevent long-term complications (retinal damage, cataracts, nerve damage, kidney damage, *hypertension, heart attack, stroke,* or death). Diabetics must *inject* insulin approximately four times a day, follow a regimented diet, and exercise to avoid complications. Injecting too much

insulin, which results in hypoglycemia (a lack of sugar in the blood), can lead to dizziness, confusion, unconsciousness, and *seizures*. Diabetics are advised to carry a sugar source to counteract an insulin *overdose* should the need arise.

Scientists believe that diabetes mellitus is caused by a combination of environmental and hereditary factors. The condition can remain hidden for years, but some things—including obesity, pancreatitis, some *drugs*, infections, and pregnancy—can cause it to manifest.

Diet Aid

Any *drug* taken to help suppress appetite. Many of these drugs can be bought *over the counter,* but some require a *prescription.* Diet aids are taken orally, as a pill, gum, or a lozenge.

Two main active ingredients are found in over-the-counter diet aids. Phenylpropanolamine, a *stimulant* similar to *amphetamines,* is used as both an appetite suppressant and a *decongestant.* It increases *heart* rate, suppresses appetite, and provides additional energy. Negative *side effects* may include dry mouth, nausea, headache, *hallucinations,* anxiety, and insomnia. People with *hypertension* should avoid this drug; dangerous complications may occur, especially *stroke.* Diet aids with phenylpropanolamine may help with weight loss when taken in conjunction with a low-calorie diet and exercise, but the effects usually stop after a month or so.

Benzocaine is a local *anesthetic* similar to *novocaine.* By numbing the taste buds, Benzocaine makes eating less pleasurable, thus helping users to cut down on the amount of food they eat. This drug often comes in lozenge form and is placed under the tongue before meals. Benzocaine can cause allergic reactions, resulting in rash, closure of airways, circulatory difficulties, or death.

Prescription diet aids affect the levels of certain neurotransmitters in the *central nervous system,* particularly *serotonin,* which affects mood and appetite. Reactions to these drugs differ, and they may not help all people. Weight loss usually occurs in the first six months of use. It is not advised to stay on them for longer than a year. Some prescription diet aids, particularly dexfenfluramine, have been taken off the market because of heart valve complications that may arise from use.

Dilaudid

Dilaudid

The brand name of the *opioid analgesic* hydromorphone. Similar to *morphine,* Dilaudid is prescribed to treat moderate to severe coughing and severe pain from burns, *cancer, heart attack,* injury, and surgery. Dilaudid is seven to ten times more powerful than morphine and begins acting sooner. It does not last as long, however, and results in less nausea and vomiting. Dilaudid is more likely than morphine to lead to difficulty in breathing. It comes in pill, syrup, and intravenous form.

Dilaudid has a long list of negative *side effects:* constipation, drowsiness, difficulty in thinking, mood swings, nausea, vomiting, troubled breathing, and anxiety. Less common side effects include blurred vision, chills, cramps, rashes, diarrhea, difficulty urinating, disorientation, *depression,* lightheadedness, fainting, *hallucinations,* headache, insomnia, blood pressure fluctuations, tremors, *cardiac arrhythmia,* dizziness, sweating, and numbness. Large *doses* may cause slowed breathing. Dilaudid increases the effects of *alcohol* and could lead to dangerous complications, including death. An *overdose* of Dilaudid can cause bluish, cold, and clammy skin; sluggishness; labored breathing; weakness; *low blood pressure;* slow *heart* rate; heart attack; *coma;* and death.

Taking Dilaudid regularly can lead to *physical* and *psychological dependence* in as soon as a few days. *Tolerance* can develop quickly, and *withdrawal* symptoms are similar to those of morphine.

Distilled Alcohol

Alcohol made primarily from fermented grains or fruits. The grain or fruit is crushed and mixed with water. The mixture is then heated to boiling. The vapors from the boiling mixture are collected, forming a liquid—distilled alcohol.

The amount of alcohol in a distilled drink is that drink's "proof." In the United States, a drink's proof is twice the amount of alcohol contained in it (a drink that is 100 proof contains 50 percent alcohol).

Whiskey, the most popular form of distilled alcohol in the United States, is made from barley, corn, or rye. Most whiskey is from 80 to 100 proof. Vodka, a colorless alcohol, is made from barley, corn, rye, or potatoes, and varies from 80 to 100 proof. Other forms of distilled alcohol include liqueur, rum, brandy, and cognac.

DMT

Dimethyltryptamine is a *hallucinogen* similar to, but not as popular as, *LSD.* DMT occurs naturally in the seeds and bark of some South American trees and has a long history as a hallucinogenic snuff and drink used by the native Indians. DMT can also be made *synthetically.* It is usually *smoked* but can also be *snorted* and *injected.* A DMT *high* is powerful and begins within seconds of consumption. Unlike that of LSD, which lasts for eight to twelve hours, a DMT high lasts for about thirty minutes, earning the nickname "businessman's trip."

The effects of DMT are very similar to those of LSD and *psilocybin* but can be more powerful and frightening. *Side effects* include dry mouth, dilated pupils, nausea, vomiting, anxiety, increased blood pressure, increased pulse, laughing, *hallucinations,* hallucinations while eyes are closed (called the "kaleidoscope effect"), difficulty talking, relaxation, difficulty in concentrating, excitability, panic, *cardiac arrhythmia,* and extreme paranoia. The greatest danger associated with DMT are accidents (sometimes fatal) that occur when the user loses control or believes he or she can do things that defy reality. DMT is not believed to cause *chemical dependence,* but it can quickly lead to *tolerance.* Usually the first use is the most intense.

Unlike LSD and psilocybin, DMT is not frequently used as a "party drug" because it acts so quickly and does not last very long (users report feeling as if they were high for hours). DMT often results in bad *trips* because of the sudden loss of control it induces. Users often feel dislocated from reality or transported to a new reality, sometimes depicted as a brief encounter with insanity. Most drug users who take DMT are experienced hallucinogen users, not *experimental* drug users.

Dopamine

A neurotransmitter (chemical messenger) in the *central nervous system* similar to *adrenaline.* Dopamine affects the way we feel pleasure and pain. It also affects the processes that control movement.

Some *drugs* raise the level of dopamine in the brain, stimulating feelings of *euphoria* and excitement. When these drugs leave the body, the amount of dopamine in the brain drops off, causing the individual to experience a *crash.*

Some drugs, like *cocaine,* achieve a *high* by preventing dopamine from passing on from the synapse between neurons (the messenger cells of the central nervous system) by binding to dopamine *receptors.* Others, like

61

Dose

See also:
Date-Rape Drug

amphetamines, stimulate the neurons and increase the amount of dopamine in the brain. Both processes can lead to drug *tolerance* if allowed to continue for a period of time. *Withdrawal* symptoms occur when a person addicted to these drugs tries to quit because the dopamine levels in the brain remain very low without the drugs.

Dose

The amount of a *drug* taken at a specified time. Dosage is expressed in several ways. Weight is most frequently measured in milligrams. Volume of liquids is measured in milliliters. Dose can also be measured in regard to its effects on the body, usually expressed in number of pills, capsules, drops, etc.

It is very important to follow dosage instructions with all drugs. Taking too little of a drug may render it ineffective. Taking too much may result in an *overdose*. Similar complications can occur when the drug is taken at the wrong time or taken too often. Patients are advised to follow their doctor's instructions when taking *prescription drugs*. When taking *over-the-counter drugs*, persons should read and follow the directions and precautions on the package to avoid dangerous complications.

The term "dose" can also refer to giving a drug to a person surreptitiously, either by putting it in food or drink or by replacing one drug with another that might have a different effect. This is a dangerous action that can result in serious consequences. For example, some people prey on unsuspecting women by placing mood-altering drugs in their drinks in order to sexually assault them. This type of action is subject to criminal prosecution.

A dose can be measured by the number of pills to be taken at a specific time.

See also:
Drug Abuse
Drug Interaction
FDA
Gateway Drug
Hard Drug
Pharmacodynamics
Pharmacokinetics
Soft Drug

Drug

A chemical that modifies the way the body and its organs work or hinders the way an illness affects the body. Types of drugs include *prescription drugs*, *over-the-counter drugs*, *recreational drugs*, and illegal drugs. Drugs are categorized in three ways: by chemical components, by the illness they treat, or by their effects on the body, which can be positive or negative.

Drugs can be taken in several forms: as a pill, capsule, tablet, syrup, or liquid (orally); as a suppository (via the anus); by *injection* into a vein or muscle; or by *smoking*. Medically, the drug *dose* often depends on the ailment or the severity of the condition. Taking too much of any drug can result in *overdose*.

Many drugs, such as *marijuana* and *penicillin*, occur naturally in plants, animals, molds, and other substances. *Synthetic drugs*, such as *LSD*, are made in laboratories. Some drug categories contain substances that are both found in nature and manufactured, such as *opiates* and *nicotine*. Modern scientists have discovered countless ways to replicate natural substances and create new drugs—legal and illegal.

Drugs act by influencing the cells of the body. Some attach themselves to *receptors* in the *central nervous system*. Others alter the chemical activity within cells. Drugs called *placebos* affect the user's mental outlook, without necessarily making a physical change in the body. When drugs enter the body, they are carried to different organs via the bloodstream. The body eliminates drugs primarily through the *kidneys* and urine.

Drug Abuse

The use of a *drug*—legal or illegal—for a purpose other than that for which it was initially prescribed or suggested. The term generally applies to a practice that is considered improper or dysfunctional by society, although it does not necessarily include drug *addiction*. Drug abuse can be the *experimental* use of *recreational drugs;* the use of legal drugs (in a manner in which they were not intended to be used) to relieve personal problems or to achieve an altered physical or mental state; or the compulsive use of a drug resulting in *physical* or *psychological dependence*.

Drug abuse occurs in all levels of the population and all walks of life. It is not merely a problem found in cites and in areas of low socioeconomic circumstances. Drug abuse does not involve only illegal drugs. *Prescription drugs* can pose a large problem with regard to experimentation, improper use, and addiction.

Some common drugs of abuse are *stimulants, anabolic steroids, depressants, alcohol, opiates, marijuana, LSD,* prescription drugs, and even *over-the-counter drugs*. Few drugs have no potential for abuse. Drug abuse can ultimately lead to physical, mental, emotional, social, and familial problems. The signs of drug abuse are numerous; they may include *depression*, anxiety, talkativeness, lethargy, aggressive behavior, sudden changes in behavior or personality, poor school and/or work performance, and insomnia.

Drug Interaction

Changes in a *drug*'s effect on the body from the presence of a second drug or a food. Sometimes these interactions are beneficial; most often, however, they are harmful. Drug interactions can result from mixing *prescription drugs, over-the-counter drugs,* social drugs, and illegal drugs.

There are several forms of drug interaction. Two drugs with similar properties can cause the reactions to intensify. *Side effects* can be dangerous, for example, when one mixes two *depressants,* such as *alcohol* and *barbiturates.*

Drugs with opposite effects can cancel each other out. People with chest colds should avoid *cough remedies* that contain both expectorants (drugs that help bring up fluids from the lungs through coughing) and suppressants (drugs that inhibit the cough reflex) because they negate each other.

Sometimes food can hamper a drug's effectiveness. Some forms of *penicillin* do not work well when taken after eating because the food prevents them from being absorbed from the stomach and small intestine into the bloodstream.

The *liver* acts to change the structure of (or metabolize) drugs as they pass through it so they can be eliminated from the body by the *kidneys.* Some drugs either speed up or slow down the liver's functioning, thus causing other drugs to be metabolized too quickly or too slowly. For example, *nicotine* can speed up the action of the liver, making some *analgesics* less effective. In addition, some drugs can affect the rate at which the kidneys eliminate waste from the body, thus causing other drugs to remain in the system too long.

To avoid dangerous drug interactions, always check with your physician before mixing drugs, and always reveal all drugs you are currently taking before your physician prescribes new drugs.

Drug Rehabilitation

The process of helping someone who is addicted to legal or illegal drugs to "kick the habit" through a variety of programs and treatments. *Drug* treatments include counseling (one-on-one, small group, large group), psychotherapy, family counseling sessions, medical treatment, *detoxification,* job and life-skills seminars, and *twelve-step programs* such as *Alcoholics Anonymous* and *Narcotics Anonymous.*

The purpose of drug treatment is to end *addiction* to drugs and *alcohol,* regardless of how the person undergoing treatment feels about it. Some

people require strong persuasion to enter drug-treatment programs and/or facilities; effective treatment is not necessarily voluntary. Sometimes that persuasion comes in the form of family and/or friend *intervention,* employer mandate, or criminal prosecution.

No single treatment plan is appropriate for everyone. Effective drug treatment must meet multiple criteria and usually addresses medical and psychological problems as well as work-related and legal obstacles. *Recovery* from drug addiction is often a long process involving multiple methods of treatment and numerous treatment sessions. *Relapse* is common among heavy drug users, and treatment should be systematically monitored, assessed, and modified to ensure a greater probability of success. Monitoring methods include frequent counseling sessions and periodic *drug testing.* In addition to formal drug-treatment programs, individuals should be encouraged to attend self-help or twelve-step programs, which enable them to monitor their own progress with the aid and support of others with similar addictions. The duration of treatment programs depends on the specific situation and progress, but most treatments last from three months to a year.

Drug Testing

Also called drug screening, drug testing includes several methods of determining if someone (often an employee) has been using such *drugs* as *marijuana, cocaine, amphetamines, opiates, barbiturates,* and *alcohol.* This is done for safety and legal reasons. Some companies test candidates for drugs before hiring them. Others have random drug tests throughout the year. Professional, amateur, and high school athletes are sometimes tested for drugs, including performance-enhancing drugs such as *anabolic steroids.*

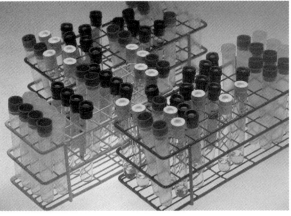

The main types of drug tests are blood, urine, and hair; less common tests include saliva and fingernail tests. Hair tests are the least dependable. They can detect long-term drug use but not recent use (in the previous week) and are not affected by temporary *abstinence.* Urine tests are perhaps the most common, but they can be beaten by abstaining from drug use a week before the test. Drinking large amounts of water prior to urine tests may affect the results. Blood tests are the most effective but the least common, perhaps because of cost.

Individuals can be drug tested for substance use and/or abuse through urine, hair, and blood tests.

See also:
Breathalyzer

Many products are available that help users beat drug tests (especially for marijuana use). These either mask the results of the test or help to flush the substance from the body before the test (in the case of urine tests). Certain shampoos help users beat hair tests. Most of these products are not 100 percent dependable.

Drug Trafficking

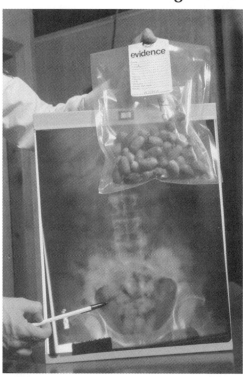

Some drug smugglers swallow drugs so that they will remain undetected in transportation.

A system of processes—including cultivation, production, transportation, and dissemination—that provide illegal *drugs* to locations around the world. Most drug trafficking was once primarily an internal problem (run by organized crime families, prison gangs, motorcycle gangs, and other violent groups), but it is now a problem that often originates in foreign countries. Drugs are produced in such countries as Colombia, Mexico, Nigeria, Jamaica, and the Dominican Republic and smuggled into the United States by planes, ships, trucks, and other means. At that point the drugs pass along a chain of *dealers* to be sold on a local level.

The *DEA* struggles to contain drug trafficking year after year. It sometimes works with foreign governments to help bring drug cartel leaders to justice. But drug trafficking groups have become exceedingly violent in the past twenty years, and many are considered terrorists. Since drug trafficking generates millions of dollars a year, the cartels often have modern, high-tech equipment with which to conduct business, including planes, ships, communications devices, and weapons. This makes it harder and more dangerous for American authorities to stop them. In addition, when one group of drug traffickers is broken up, another quickly takes its place.

DWI

Driving while intoxicated (sometimes DUI, or driving under the influence) is a criminal charge filed against someone who is arrested for driving a motor vehicle while *intoxicated* on *alcohol.* In the United States, over 20 percent of all traffic fatalities are caused by drunk drivers.

The DWI laws of every state but two (Massachusetts and North Carolina) make it a crime to drive with a *blood alcohol level* (BAL) at or above the legal level for that state, but the laws differ from state to state. In most states, drivers are convicted of DWI if their BAL is at or above .10 percent, although the level in many states is .08 percent. The level for minors (usually people under twenty-one) in most states is .02 percent. In October 2000, a federal law was enacted requiring all states to meet the .08 BAL within four years or suffer the loss of federal funds. In most states, a first-time DWI conviction results in the suspension of the driver's license for one month to a year, depending on the state. Fines for drunk driving range from $500 to $1,000. Presently, fourteen states have mandatory jail or community-service time for first offenders. Repeat offenders face stiffer jail sentences and fines, in addition to the suspension or revocation of their driver's license.

Forty states and Washington, DC have a DWI law called administrative license suspension. This means that law enforcement authorities can immediately suspend a driver's license if the person fails or refuses to take a *Breathalyzer* test.

- Ecstasy
- Emphysema
- Endorphins
- Ephedrine
- Ergot
- Ether
- Euphoria
- Experimentation

Ecstasy

See *MDMA*.

Emphysema

A disease characterized by difficulty in breathing because of damaged alveoli (tiny air sacs in the *lungs*). Emphysema causes deterioration of the usually rigid walls of the alveoli, resulting in narrowed air passages and labored breathing. In addition, large pockets of carbon dioxide form inside the lungs, obstructing the natural flow of oxygen and carbon dioxide that occurs during respiration. This disease may develop for years unobserved. Emphysema is one form of chronic obstructive pulmonary disease (obstruction of the airways); the other is chronic *bronchitis.*

Emphysema is essentially caused by the release of *toxic* enzymes into the bloodstream that destroy the alveoli walls. A body chemical called alpha1-antitrypsin prevents these enzymes from damaging the alveoli. Some people have a deficiency of alpha1-antitrypsin (a hereditary condition) and as a result develop emphysema. The number one cause of emphysema, however, is *cigarette smoking*, which also prohibits alpha1-antitrypsin from functioning correctly. Other factors that may play a role in the development of emphysema include air pollution and infections.

The symptoms of emphysema include shortness of breath, chronic bronchitis, an enlarged chest (from the trapped pockets of carbon dioxide), persistent coughing, *heart* disease, frequent colds, and a bluish skin color from lack of oxygen in the blood. Because damaged lung tissue cannot be repaired, emphysema is incurable. If it is caught soon enough, preventive measures can be taken to lengthen the patient's life. Smokers must stop smoking immediately. Some *drugs* help reduce the amount of fluid in the body, and some widen the air passages to make breathing easier. In advanced cases, death occurs eventually from *heart failure* or respiratory complications.

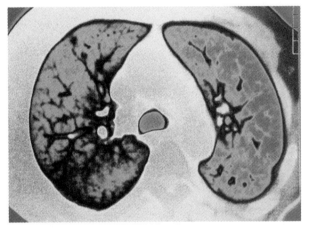

Ecstasy

Image of lungs with alveoli damage caused by emphysema.

See also:
Tobacco

Endorphins

A group of neurotransmitters (chemical messengers) in the body that relieve pain. In 1973, scientists discovered *opiate receptors* in the *central nervous system*. They soon realized that natural chemicals in the body very similar to *morphine*—endorphins—bind to the same receptors.

Endorphins act as natural *analgesics* to block pain from injury, help cope with stress, alter mood, improve memory, and slow the aging process. They also give the *immune system* a boost when it is really needed; endorphins can sometimes kill cancer cells. Endorphins provide a natural *high* in times of stress or pain, resulting in a temporary sense of *euphoria*. Runners are said to achieve this type of "endorphin high" after running long distances.

Researchers believe that *addiction* to *opioid analgesics* and the *tolerance* that accompanies it may be the result of the *narcotic*'s suppression of endorphins. When people stop using a narcotic *drug*, they experience *withdrawal* symptoms because of the absence of endorphins.

Ephedrine

A *stimulant* similar to *amphetamines* and *adrenaline* found in *decongestants, diet aids,* and bronchodilators (*drugs* that relax bronchial muscles to ease breathing). Ephedrine is believed by some to heighten athletic performance, but no solid evidence supports this notion. The drug comes in tablet or pill form and is found in some *over-the-counter* cold, allergy, and asthma medications. It can also be found in powder form.

Ephedrine provides its users with extra energy and increases alertness. It also suppresses appetite. People with asthma sometimes use it to open up the bronchial airways. Negative *side effects* include sweating, dry mouth, dizziness, anxiety, increased *heart* rate, and insomnia. More serious effects may include high blood pressure, breathing difficulty, confusion, paranoia, memory loss, muscle spasms, tremors, and *cardiac arrhythmia*. Larger *doses* of the drug do not necessarily affect the body twice as much as a single dose, although deaths have been linked to abnormally large doses (ten to twelve pills with eight milligrams of ephedrine each). People with heart conditions, *diabetes,* or high blood pressure should not take ephedrine.

Derived from the ma huang plant found in China, ephedrine can produce a feeling of *euphoria*. Ephedrine is found in a number of abused substances, particularly *herbal stimulants,* and can be particularly harmful when mixed with other stimulants such as *caffeine*.

Ergot

A fungus that causes a disease in rye and other cereals. Although ergot is a strong *poison,* it is valued for its medical benefits, particularly as a medication for Parkinson's disease. Parkinson's disease is a slowly degenerative disease of the *central nervous system* characterized by rigid muscles and shaking. It is caused by a deficiency of the neurotransmitter *dopamine.* *Prescription drugs* containing ergot, particularly bromocriptine, help increase levels of dopamine in the central nervous system, easing the negative effects of Parkinson's disease, at least for a few years.

While experimenting with ergot, scientists discovered a derivative called *LSD,* a *hallucinogenic drug.* Instead of affecting dopamine, however, LSD enhances the neurotransmitter *serotonin.*

Ether

The first general *anesthetic.* Ether, a colorless liquid that produces unconsciousness when inhaled, has been used in a medical capacity since 1275, but it was not used as an anesthetic until the early 1840s. Although ether is generally safe to use, it is highly flammable, and even static electricity can make it explode. Ether was used commonly in surgery until the 1930s but has been replaced by safer anesthesia.

Ether was used for years as a component of *freebase cocaine.* It was extremely dangerous, however, because the ingredients (ether and ammonia) are highly flammable, and frequent accidents occurred while preparing and *smoking* the *drug.* A modern equivalent of ether freebase cocaine is *crack,* which is a freebase form of cocaine mixed with sodium bicarbonate (the active ingredient in baking soda) instead of ether.

Euphoria

Intense feelings of well-being and confidence. Euphoria can occur naturally as a result of personal achievements, as with winning an athletic competition or getting a promotion at work. Certain injuries and illnesses can also cause euphoria, especially head injuries, brain tumors, and multiple sclerosis.

Many *drugs* cause users to feel euphoric. Certain drugs increase levels of neurotransmitters (chemical messengers) in the *central nervous system,* altering the way a person feels. Certain neurotransmitters increase confidence and happiness, sometimes to the point of blissful emotions. Some drugs increase the levels of neurotransmitters in the brain (as *cocaine* does

with the neurotransmitter *dopamine*) and *synthetically* create feelings of euphoria. When the drug leaves the body, however, the person often experiences a *crash* as the level of neurotransmitter drops off drastically. This situation often leads to *physical* and *psychological dependence* as the user takes more and more of the substance to achieve euphoria and avoid the crash.

Experimentation

The act of trying a substance (or trying *drugs* and *alcohol* in general) for the first time to see how it affects the body. The term "experimentation" implies a willingness to try new things, a youthful recklessness, and/or a sense of innocence about the effects of one's actions. Certain substances are typically used to experiment with drug use, particularly *marijuana* and alcohol. These drugs are considered *gateway drugs* because they often lead to the use of *hard drugs*. Any drug, however, can be considered experimental when the user has never taken it before, regardless of how "experienced" he or she is with drugs and alcohol.

All *recreational drug* users begin at the experimental stage. It is initiated for several reasons, including a sense of curiosity or adventure, lack of education about the substance, *peer pressure* and/or the desire to "fit in," and psychological problems such as *depression* and anxiety. Experimentation for some may be merely a passing inclination; for others it can lead to serious health and social consequences, including *physical* and *psychological dependence, overdose,* poor work/school performance, loss of friends, familial confrontations, and a long list of physical illnesses.

F

- FDA
- Fentanyl
- Fermented Alcohol
- Fetal Alcohol Syndrome
- Flashback
- Freebase

FDA

The Food and Drug Administration is a government consumer protection agency that regulates food, *prescription* and *over-the-counter drugs,* medical products, the national blood supply, cosmetics, animal feed and drugs, and

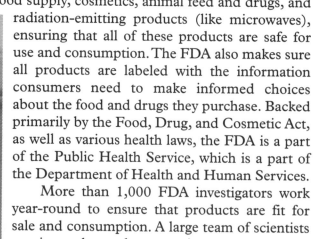

radiation-emitting products (like microwaves), ensuring that all of these products are safe for use and consumption. The FDA also makes sure all products are labeled with the information consumers need to make informed choices about the food and drugs they purchase. Backed primarily by the Food, Drug, and Cosmetic Act, as well as various health laws, the FDA is a part of the Public Health Service, which is a part of the Department of Health and Human Services.

More than 1,000 FDA investigators work year-round to ensure that products are fit for sale and consumption. A large team of scientists continuously conduct experiments on new and old products to ensure that they meet standards. Some 3,000 products are taken off the market each year because the FDA has determined that they are unfit for sale. The FDA regulates approximately $1 trillion worth of products every year.

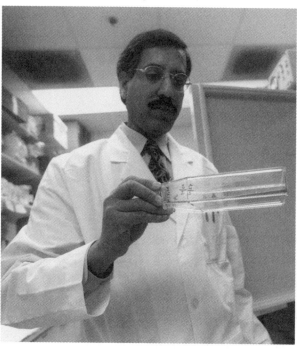

A doctor in the FDA performs tests on cells to check the effectiveness of a drug.

Fentanyl

A *synthetic opioid analgesic* that is 50 to 100 times more potent than *morphine* but does not last as long. Fentanyl is used as a general *anesthetic* during surgery and is preferred to morphine because it is safer for the *heart.* It is prescribed to alleviate chronic pain from injury and *cancer.* Veterinarians also prescribe fentanyl as a pain reliever for dogs and cats. The *drug* can be taken intravenously, transdermally (through the skin via a patch), or orally in the form of a lozenge.

Fentanyl is a *depressant* that relieves pain and produces unconsciousness. Other *side effects* include dry mouth, sweating, rash, headache, constipation, nausea, vomiting, *depression,* anxiety, drowsiness, respiratory depression, *low blood pressure, hallucinations,* confusion, mood swings, *euphoria, cardiac arrhythmia,* bad dreams, memory loss, and tremors. An *overdose* of fentanyl can result in dizziness, *seizures,*

unconsciousness, *coma,* and death. This drug should not be mixed with *alcohol, tranquilizers,* or *antihistamines.*

Fentanyl can result in *physical* and *psychological dependence* after prolonged use. Upon halting its use, a person may experience the following *withdrawal* symptoms: diarrhea, increased heartbeat, fever, runny nose, profuse sweating, nausea, vomiting, loss of appetite, restlessness, irritability, trembling, stomach cramps, and insomnia.

Fentanyl has been known to be abused by medical professionals because it is easy to find in hospitals. It has also generated great concern as the basis for *designer drugs.* Fentanyl analogs, the first of which was China White, are very similar to *heroin* but far more potent and deadly. These derivatives of fentanyl are often considered *club drugs* and can be found at raves or all-night dance parties. Negative effects of fentanyl derivatives include depressed respiration, respiratory paralysis, and sudden death. Fentanyl analogs can be *injected, smoked,* or *snorted.*

Fermented Alcohol

Alcohol made by adding yeast to certain substances that contain sugar. Yeast causes sugar to ferment, which changes the sugar into ethyl alcohol and carbon dioxide gas.

Beer is a carbonated fermented alcohol made primarily from barley malt. Beer usually contains between 2 and 6 percent alcohol. Most beers have a golden color, but some are dark brown or even black in color.

Wine is primarily made from grapes but can also be made from apples, cherries, or other fruits. Winemakers crush the fruit and then ferment the juice. Most wine has an alcohol content between 7 and 24 percent. Wine can be red, white, or pink, and either dry or sweet.

Other types of fermented alcohol include ale, hard cider, and sake, a Japanese drink made from fermented rice.

Fetal Alcohol Syndrome (FAS)

Also known as ARBD (*alcohol*-related *birth defects),* fetal alcohol syndrome is a condition in some infants born to mothers who drank excessive amounts of alcohol during *pregnancy.* Small amounts of alcohol may not cause birth defects, but FAS results when pregnant women drink large amounts of alcohol or are *binge drinkers.* Fetal alcohol effect (FAE) is a less severe version of the same condition.

Infants with FAS can develop a wide variety of mental and physical defects: chronic illness, low birth weight, small body and body parts (especially the head, indicating poor brain development), malformed facial features, hearing and visual problems, *heart* defects, *central nervous system* defects, *immune system* defects, hyperactivity, difficulty in learning and concentrating, mental retardation, epilepsy, cerebral palsy, *kidney* failure, *heart failure*, and death.

Alcohol consumption during pregnancy is the number one preventable cause of mental retardation. Approximately 30 to 40 percent of babies born to mothers who drank during pregnancy have FAS; approximately 5,000 infants are born each year with FAS. There is no cure for FAS, but it is preventable simply by avoiding alcohol during pregnancy.

Flashback

A situation experienced by persons who frequently use *hallucinogens* (especially *LSD*). During a flashback, the person feels as if he or she is "tripping" (*high* on a hallucinogen), even though not currently using a hallucinogen. These instances are usually not as intense as the original high but can seem like a frightening loss of control. Flashbacks are categorized in three groups: emotional (characterized by intense feelings of panic, fear, and loneliness), somatic (physical reactions like tremors, nausea, and dizziness), and perceptual (sensory distortions and *hallucinations*).

Drugs such as *marijuana* and *alcohol* can trigger flashbacks, as can stress, exercise, fatigue, and anxiety. Flashbacks can happen weeks, months, or years after using a hallucinogenic drug, but they are rare.

Children born with fetal alcohol syndrome can develop a variety of physical and mental defects.

Freebase

The process of purifying *cocaine* to make a more powerful *drug* for *smoking*. Making freebase cocaine entails mixing cocaine powder with water, ammonia, and *ether*. The ether is removed from the mixture and set aside to evaporate. When it does, white crystals are left over; this is freebase. The freebase is allowed to dry completely and is placed in a *pipe* to be smoked. The *high* from smoking cocaine is more intense than from *snorting* or *injecting* it. Cocaine has *anesthetic* qualities, and smoking it can scorch the *lungs* without the user's knowing it. Freebasing is also believed to be more addictive and makes the user more aggressive and paranoid than snorting or injecting.

Creating freebase cocaine can be as dangerous as smoking it. Ammonia is a *volatile solvent* and can be harmful if touched or inhaled. Ether is a strong anesthetic and can cause unconsciousness if inhaled. Ether is also highly flammable, and many people have died from explosions when making freebase cocaine. *Crack* is a freebase form of cocaine that was invented by *dealers* as a safer form of the drug. Crack is mixed with sodium bicarbonate (the active ingredient in baking soda) instead of ammonia and ether.

Freebase

- Gateway Drug
- GHB
- Glue Sniffing
- Glutethimide

Gateway Drug

A *drug* that leads to the use of other, often more harmful, drugs. Some researchers believe, for example, that *smoking marijuana* can lead to the abuse of *hard drugs.* This may be a result of an *addictive personality;* but also, smoking marijuana may cause higher levels of certain chemicals to develop within the brain. These chemicals build up in times of stress, perhaps leading to a greater desire to alter one's perceptions and emotions with the aid of drugs.

Research is ongoing in this area. Although people with addictive personalities may be more likely to develop *cross-drug addictions*—and some may like to *experiment* more than others—it still is not clear if one drug can cause an individual to start using other drugs. Many researchers think that the connections between gateway drugs (*inhalants, cigarettes, alcohol,* and marijuana) and harder drugs (*cocaine, heroin,* and *hallucinogens*) may be the result of patterns of behavior, and not necessarily the drugs themselves.

There does seem to be a connection, however, between *nicotine* and *alcohol.* A majority of people addicted to alcohol are also addicted to nicotine, but the reason for the relationship has not yet been discovered.

GHB

Gamma-hydroxy-butrate, a natural metabolite found in mammals, is closely related to the neurotransmitter (chemical messenger) GABA (gamma-aminobutyric acid). GABA is the most common neurotransmitter in the *central nervous system;* it keeps the system functioning properly by affecting the release of other neurotransmitters, especially *dopamine.*

First derived *synthetically* from GABA in the early 1960s, GHB was initially used as an *anesthetic.* It has since been used to treat insomnia, narcolepsy (sudden daytime sleep), Parkinson's disease (characterized by rigid muscles and shaking), and schizophrenia. It also has been used as a childbirth aid, to ease the effects of alcohol *withdrawal,* as an *antianxiety drug,* and more recently to increase growth hormone levels. GHB has also been found to lower cholesterol and improve memory. GHB is a clear liquid and can be taken orally or intravenously.

GHB is a *depressant* comparable to *alcohol,* causing a drunken feeling, but lacking alcohol's tendency to cause stupor. Studies of the *drug* present contradictions concerning its effects and safety. Some researchers insist that GHB is primarily harmless, lacks negative *side effects* (such as *physical dependence* and *tolerance),* and is a valuable medical tool. Others report that it is a dangerous social drug and can result in dizziness, nausea, vomiting,

cardiac arrhythmia, depressed respiration, *seizures,* and *physical* and *psychological dependence.*

Known facts about the drug are that it can cause sedation and *euphoria* in small *doses* and amnesia in large doses. A GHB *overdose* is not believed to be exceedingly harmful, although it can result in deep unconsciousness. For this reason, GHB has been abused as a *date-rape drug* and is illegal in several states. Some people abuse GHB for its alcohol-like effects. Some studies have reported *withdrawal* symptoms, including anxiety, insomnia, muscle pains, and trouble concentrating.

Glue Sniffing

See *Inhalant* and *Volatile Solvent.*

Glutethimide

A *hypnotic-sedative* that was once commonly used to treat insomnia but has been replaced by safer, less addictive *drugs.* Glutethimide and methaqualone *(Quaalude)* were developed in the 1960s as *barbiturate* alternatives but were found to be more dangerous and addictive. Glutethimide is usually taken orally.

Like all *depressants,* glutethimide causes sedation and can reduce anxiety. Negative *side effects* include rash, fever, weakness, blurred vision, uncoordinated movements, dizziness, nausea, and vomiting. Higher *doses* can result in unconsciousness, respiratory depression, *heart failure, coma,* and death. A glutethimide *overdose,* or mixing it with other *central nervous system* depressants like *codeine* or barbiturates, can be more difficult to treat than barbiturate overdose and can result in slurred speech, bluish skin, fever, confusion, weakness, troubled breathing, slow heartbeat, *cardiac arrhythmia,* memory loss, muscle spasms, *seizures,* coma, and death.

This drug can cause *physical* and *psychological dependence* in as little as seven days and should not be used for chronic sleeping problems. Users can also develop a *tolerance* for glutethimide. *Withdrawal* symptoms may include fast heartbeat, *hallucinations,* nightmares, nausea, vomiting, stomach cramps, seizures, and trouble sleeping.

- Hallucination
- Hallucinogen
- Hangover
- Hard Drug
- Hashish/Hash Oil
- Hazing
- Heart (effects of drugs on)
- Heart Attack
- Heart Failure
- Hepatitis
- Herbal Stimulant
- Heroin
- High
- HIV
- Homegrown
- Huffing
- Hydrocodone
- Hypertension
- Hypnotic-Sedative

Hallucination

Hallucination

A state in which a person sees or hears something that is not actually present. Hallucinations can also occur with the other senses (taste, smell, and touch) but are very rare. Auditory hallucinations are the most common.

Certain Native American groups use the hallucinogen peyote in religious rituals.

See also:
Delirium Tremens

Hallucinations are usually a sign of mental disorder. People with schizophrenia and manic-depressive disorder often report hearing voices. People suffering from delirium sometimes think they see things that are not really there. People suffering from extreme physical conditions may also have hallucinations, including those subjected to sensory deprivation (a state of being removed from all sensory stimulus, as with some prisoners in solitary confinement) and those subjected to intense physical stress or illness (as *pneumonia*).

Particular *drugs* can cause hallucinations. *Hallucinogens*—psychedelic drugs, including *LSD, psilocybin,* and *mescaline*—cause hallucinations in addition to other *side effects*. These hallucinations may entail a crossover of the senses; for example, someone listening to music may believe they see colors or shapes moving in time to the beat. They are called pseudo or false hallucinations because the people who experience them generally know they are not real. People sometimes take these drugs with the intention of experiencing hallucinations, but an experience of this kind can be quite frightening and is sometimes known as a "bad *trip*."

Hallucinations may be caused by *marijuana* and *inhalants*, by *alcohol withdrawal*, and even by certain *prescription drugs*.

Hallucinogen

A *drug* that produces *hallucinations*. Hallucinogenic drugs include *LSD, peyote, mescaline,* and *psilocybin*. Depending on the drug, the effects may begin within thirty minutes to an hour and can last six to twelve hours or longer. Other drugs may also have hallucinogenic effects, including *marijuana, alcohol* (during *withdrawal*), and certain *prescription drugs*.

Hallucinogens disrupt neurotransmitters (chemical messengers) in the *central nervous system,* altering the way one perceives the world. In addition to hallucinations, hallucinogens cause restlessness, dilated pupils, increased *heart* rate, mood swings, anxiety, panic, paranoia, *euphoria, depression,* a distorted view of reality, loss of control, violent behavior, and psychotic episodes. These drugs tend to intensify emotions; if someone is depressed before taking a hallucinogen, he or she is apt to be more depressed afterward. People who take hallucinogens—especially inexperienced users who are not prepared for the effects—may have a "bad *trip.*" A bad trip can result in extreme paranoia and psychotic behavior that may last for days after the drug wears off. These episodes are particularly frightening because it takes six or more hours for most hallucinogens to wear off. The best remedy for a bad trip is to spend time in quiet surroundings with people the individual trusts.

Hallucinogens do not normally lead to *overdose*-related deaths. Their use, however, can indirectly cause death, especially accidental deaths triggered by unrealistic beliefs and dangerous behavior (believing you can fly or cross a busy street without getting hurt). Chronic use may cause permanent brain damage, mental confusion, impaired memory skills, learning disabilities, *flashbacks,* suicide, *psychological dependence,* and *tolerance. Drug rehabilitation* for hallucinogen abuse may include counseling and group therapy.

Hangover

Unpleasant physical aftereffects sometimes experienced upon waking up the morning after drinking a large quantity of *alcohol.* Characteristics of a hangover include headache, stomach cramps, nausea, vomiting, dizziness, dehydration, fatigue, irritability, and *depression.* Alcoholics may experience more aggressive cases of hangover because of the related *withdrawal* symptoms.

While all alcohol can produce a hangover, the severity of the symptoms depends on the amount consumed, the time in which it was consumed, and the type of alcohol. People who *sober* up before going to bed are less likely to wake up with a hangover. Hangovers can last a few hours or most of the day.

There is no surefire way to avoid a hangover other than not drinking or drinking in moderation. The best remedy is rest. Since alcohol is a diuretic (a substance that removes larger-than-normal amounts of water from the body in the form of urine), drinking several glasses of water before bed may

See also:
Alcoholism

help ease the effects of a hangover. Taking *aspirin* or *acetaminophen* before bed has also been known to lessen the symptoms of hangovers. (Caution: It is not recommended to mix any *drug* with alcohol, as it can result in dangerous complications. Mixing acetaminophen and alcohol has been shown to cause irreversible *liver* damage.)

Other drugs have been known to cause symptoms similar to an alcohol hangover. For instance, *marijuana* smokers have reported fatigue, headaches, and depression the morning after using the drug.

Hard Drug

A general term for *drugs* that are believed to be more harmful than others. *Heroin, cocaine, methamphetamine,* and *PCP* are commonly considered hard drugs, which supposedly lead to physical and mental damage more often than so-called *soft drugs.* They also lead to *overdose* and death more often than soft drugs.

The boundary between soft drugs and hard drugs is hazy at best. Some so-called soft drugs, such as *alcohol,* can lead to the same results as hard drugs (*physical* and *psychological dependence, tolerance,* overdose, or death). *Tobacco,* for instance, may be considered a soft drug by many, but *cigarettes* are the single largest cause of *lung* cancer in the United States. Many *drug abuse* experts believe that by categorizing drugs as soft or hard, we are designating which drugs are okay for young people to *experiment* with and which should be avoided altogether. In truth, all drugs can be harmful if taken in large enough quantities or for an extended period of time.

Hashish/Hash Oil

See also:
THC

Hashish, or hash, is a tarry resin made from *marijuana.* Marijuana leaves, stems, and flowers are pressed and rolled, often by hand, until a dark, sticky by-product is left. After a great deal of work, this substance is gathered together into different sized chunks, usually square bricks. It is then broken into smaller pieces and *smoked* in a *pipe* or taken orally. Hash does not burn as easily as marijuana but is often more potent.

Hash oil is the thick, sticky liquid collected from heating and pressing hashish. Similar to *freebase cocaine,* hash oil can be made by heating hashish, water, and *ether.* The ether is extracted and allowed to evaporate, leaving behind hash oil. (This process is extremely dangerous; ether is highly flammable, and explosions are common when preparing hash oil.) Hash oil is heated and inhaled; it does not burn like marijuana and hashish, and it produces vapors, not smoke. It is sometimes used to coat *cigarette* papers and then smoked with *tobacco* or marijuana. It can also be mixed with food and eaten. Hash oil is considerably more potent than marijuana and hashish, but it is very expensive and not very common.

Hazing

Rituals—often cruel and illegal—sometimes held by college and high school athletes, military personnel, and college fraternities when initiating new members. Hazing is an act of power over others for the simple purpose of degrading them. It may include physical abuse ("paddling," branding, excessive exercise), mental abuse (teasing, ridicule, harassment), harmful practical jokes, demeaning public displays, enforced *alcohol* stunts ("keg stands" and "funnels"), and other dangerous or humiliating activities. Hazing can also affect scholastic and work performance.

Hazing can also be good-natured and harmless, like requiring a pledge to carry your books to and from class every day for a week or staging meaningless scavenger hunts. In fact, many fraternities and sororities now have hazing guidelines. Most groups are reluctant to drop hazing altogether because it is a traditional part of the fraternity and sorority experience.

Fraternity and sorority hazing, however, has become a particularly large problem over the last decade, and some concerned parental and governmental groups are trying to have it abolished altogether. Some hazing events get out of control because of the involvement of *drugs* and alcohol. Many hazing events promote *binge drinking* and other reckless behavior, which often lead to serious accidents and even death. As a result, most states have developed antihazing legislation.

Heart (effects of drugs on)

Drugs affect the heart in different ways. *Depressants* like *barbiturates* and *narcotics* can dangerously slow the heart to the point of *cardiac arrhythmia* and *heart failure*. Depressant *withdrawal* can cause an increased heart rate. Prolonged use of *alcohol* can cause coronary heart disease (blockage of the coronary arteries), *hypertension*, heart failure, and *stroke*. *Inhalants* can cause differing results depending on the drug. Some speed up the heart rate while others slow it down, sometimes to the point of heart failure. Most can cause cardiac arrhythmia. Stimulants like *amphetamines* and *cocaine* cause the heart rate to speed up and the blood pressure to rise. These drugs have been known to cause fatal *heart attacks*, even in young, physically fit individuals. *Hallucinogens* and *PCP* may also increase heart rate.

Heart Attack

Smoking tobacco is one of the leading causes of heart disease. People who smoke are twice as likely to suffer a heart attack and are more likely to die suddenly from one. *Cigarette* smoke also increases the possibility of contracting coronary heart disease. Even *secondhand smoke* increases the risk of developing heart disease. *Marijuana* is believed to carry similar risks.

People must be careful when using *prescription* and *over-the-counter drugs* as well. Those with high blood pressure, for instance, should avoid *aspirin* because it thins the blood and may cause heart complications. Conversely, aspirin is often given to people who are having a heart attack because it helps blood pass through blocked arteries. Always check with your doctor before taking any medications, especially if you have heart problems.

Heart Attack

A heart attack (myocardial infarction) is a restriction of the flow of blood, resulting in the death of *heart* muscle from lack of oxygen. Heart attack is one of the leading causes of death in America.

Heart attacks are most often caused by clots blocking the flow of blood in the coronary artery. Other risk factors include a family history of heart disease, being male, old age, *smoking, drug* use (particularly *stimulants* like *cocaine* and *methamphetamine*), *hypertension, diabetes mellitus,* atherosclerosis (narrowing of the arteries caused by a high amount of cholesterol in the bloodstream), and lack of exercise.

The symptoms of a heart attack are pain in the chest, arms, back, and/or jaw; fatigue; anxiety; sweating; difficulty in breathing; cold and clammy skin; nausea; vomiting; and unconsciousness. These symptoms—especially chest pain, weakness, and shortness of breath—may begin a few days before the heart attack. Heart attacks can cause *cardiac arrhythmia, cardiac arrest,* and *heart failure.*

In a mild heart attack, the individual may not even notice the symptoms. Severe heart attacks can cause death suddenly, or within a few hours. Other people live up to ten years after a heart attack. Patients who survive a heart attack usually develop long-term complications, particularly heart valve damage.

Treatment for a heart attack is based on quick action. Initial treatment includes *aspirin* to help thin the blood and reduce blood clots, pain relievers (particularly *morphine* and nitroglycerine), other *drugs* to help stabilize the patient and dissolve blood clots, oxygen, and surgery. People who survive a heart attack should stop smoking, eat a healthy diet, exercise, avoid stress, and take certain *prescription drugs.*

Heart Failure

A condition characterized by the *heart*'s inability to pump enough blood to the organs, resulting in a lack of oxygen. The heart does not actually stop during heart failure. Heart failure can occur in the right or left side of the heart.

The causes of heart failure include coronary artery disease (lack of blood reaching the heart because of blocked arteries), viral infections of the heart, *diabetes, hypertension,* heart valve disease, *anemia,* overactive thyroid gland, *birth defects* involving the heart, enlarged heart, *cardiac arrhythmia, heart attack,* chronic *bronchitis, emphysema,* and excessive *alcohol* consumption.

The symptoms of heart failure include fatigue, breathing difficulty (some can breathe only while sitting up), loss of breath during simple activities, waking at night gasping for breath, fluid in the lungs, sweating, weight gain, loss of appetite, indigestion, and swollen ankles and legs.

If not treated, heart failure can become dangerous. When treated properly and promptly, however, it is not usually a life-threatening condition. Treatment focuses on the underlying cause, but it may also include hospitalization, certain medications, and surgery (as in the case of heart valve disease).

Hepatitis

Inflammation of the *liver,* sometimes resulting in permanent liver damage. Hepatitis most often results from viral infection caused by poor hygiene (such as the failure to wash hands), unprotected sex, and blood transfusions (primarily in underdeveloped nations). It can also be caused by certain chemicals and *poisons, alcoholism,* certain *drugs,* drug *overdoses (acetaminophen,* for example), and sharing needles to *inject* drugs into the body. There are two kinds of hepatitis: acute and chronic.

Acute hepatitis, the more common form, lasts for a few weeks or months. It causes *jaundice,* nausea, vomiting, flu symptoms, loss of appetite, sore muscles, and pain in the abdomen. Most cases are relatively mild and may not even be diagnosed; in fact, mild forms may not even require treatment. Acute hepatitis can become severe, however, and can result in organ damage, *coma,* and death.

Chronic hepatitis is a condition that lasts for at least six months and perhaps for many years. Again, this illness is often very mild and difficult to detect. Symptoms are the same as those of acute hepatitis; more severe cases (known as chronic active hepatitis) may result in *anemia, lung* scarring, liver failure, and *cirrhosis of the liver.*

Hepatitis

See also:
Cardiac Arrest

In both types, a liver biopsy provides the only sure diagnosis. Extreme cases are treated with drugs to reduce swelling and other symptoms, and diet is sometimes modified. Those who have hepatitis caused by drug use should *abstain* from using drugs and *alcohol*. Even when a person recovers from viral hepatitis, he or she may become a "carrier," or someone who can infect others with the illness. Hepatitis A and B are now preventable by vaccination.

Herbal Stimulant

Manufactured from plants, herbal stimulants are *drugs* that stimulate the *central nervous system,* giving the user an energy boost. Most herbal stimulants contain a mixture of *over-the-counter stimulants* (particularly *caffeine* and *ephedrine* but also *nightshade,* ginger, ginkgo, ginseng, and pennyroyal). These preparations are known to cause *intoxication;* some people take them as *diet aids,* sexual stimulants, or to increase physical performance. The most common medical uses for herbal stimulants are as a *decongestant* to treat asthma and allergies; however, these uses are highly controversial within the medical community.

Herbal stimulants are often advertised as an all-natural, safe, and legal *high.* They are considered *club drugs* and are sometimes called "herbal *ecstasy*" (their effects are similar to *MDMA,* or ecstasy). Herbal stimulants typically cause increased energy, loss of appetite, *euphoria,* a sense of increased strength, tingling sensations, intermittent "rushes" (euphoric peaks), a heightened sense of awareness, and sometimes even *hallucinations.* Negative *side effects* (usually a result of too large of a *dose*) include nervousness, irritability, dizziness, shortness of breath, insomnia, nausea, vomiting, and muscle injury. More severe side effects include *hypertension, liver* failure, *cardiac arrhythmia, heart attack, stroke,* and nerve damage. Extreme *overdoses* have resulted in death.

The effects of some herbal stimulants mimic those of the drug MDMA, or ecstasy, and are sold as "herbal ecstasy."

These products are usually safe when taken in moderation. Achieving a high on herbal stimulants, however, often entails taking larger doses and mixing products. Some users become *psychologically* and *physically dependent* on the effects, particularly those who take them for an energy boost.

Herbal stimulants continue to receive attention from the *FDA*, as well as state governments, because of the growing number of accidents and deaths that have resulted from overuse.

Heroin

High

A *synthetic opiate* derived from—but more powerful than—*morphine*. In fact, heroin is one of the strongest *narcotics*. A white or brown powder, this *drug* can be *snorted, smoked,* or *injected.*

See also:
Laam
Methadone
Naltrexone

    Heroin quickly affects the *central nervous system,* both decreasing pain and increasing sensations of pleasure. Heroin creates intense *euphoria* and generates a loss of concern for the environment around the user. When these effects disappear, the user *crashes* and strongly desires another heroin *high.* Other short-term effects include dry mouth, flushed skin and warmness, calmness, sensations of heaviness, fatigue, nausea, vomiting, itching, and low *heart* rate. More severe effects include extreme weight loss, *pneumonia, kidney* failure, fluid in the *lungs,* retinal damage, an impaired *immune system,* infection of the heart, *coma,* and death. Injecting heroin can lead to skin infections and abscesses as well as bone infections. If a person shares a needle with someone who is infected with *hepatitis* (which can lead to *cirrhosis of the liver*) or *HIV,* these diseases can be transmitted. A heroin *overdose* can result in muscle spasms, bluish skin and lips, breathing difficulty, halted breathing, constipation, stomach spasms, low heart rate, drowsiness, *seizures,* unconsciousness, coma, and death.

    Heroin leads to *physical* and *psychological dependence* in as little as two to three days. Users build a *tolerance* for it and soon need more to attain the effects they once did with smaller *doses.* Heroin *withdrawal* can be severe (resulting in frequent *relapses*), but it is not life-threatening. Withdrawal symptoms begin about four hours after the last dose, peak after thirty-six to seventy-two hours, and last from seven to ten days. Symptoms of heroin withdrawal include shivering, muscle and stomach cramps, goosebumps, hyperventilation, increased heart rate, diarrhea, insomnia, flulike symptoms, anxiety, sweating, and hot and cold flashes. Treatment for heroin *addiction* may include *maintenance drugs, detoxification,* long-term stays in treatment centers, therapy, and *twelve-step programs.*

High

The state of being *intoxicated* by a *drug.* The symptoms of a high depend on the drug, but general characteristics include *euphoria,* disorientation, sleepiness, confusion, inability to concentrate, hyperactivity, and *hallucinations.*

Appropriately named, a *crash* is the negative *side effect* of coming down from a high. The term "high" refers primarily to the effects of *smoking marijuana,* which sometimes makes users feel as if they are floating and distant from the people and objects around them.

In drug-user lingo, being high is generally used in a positive context. The opposite of a high might be a "bad *trip,*" when someone intoxicated on *hallucinogens,* particularly *LSD,* is having difficulty dealing with the experience.

HIV

Human immunodeficiency virus is an infection of the blood that gradually destroys white blood cells needed to fight infections. Eventually this leads to acquired immunodeficiency syndrome *(AIDS),* a breakdown of the body's *immune system.*

Protesters in South Africa demand affordable access to drugs used to treat people infected with HIV.

HIV is transmitted in three ways: First, HIV can be transmitted through sexual intercourse. Second, direct contact with infected blood can result in the transmission of the virus. Many people contract HIV from sharing needles used to *inject* illegal *drugs* into the body. Third, HIV can be transmitted from a pregnant mother to her unborn baby. Transmission requires contact with bodily fluids. HIV cannot be transmitted by casual contact or through the air.

Once a person has contracted HIV, the virus multiplies and destroys white blood cells called helper T lymphocytes, which activate other cells in the immune system. By destroying helper T lymphocytes, HIV prevents the body from protecting itself against infections and *cancers.*

The symptoms of HIV include fever, rash, and swollen lymph nodes. These symptoms may last for about two weeks after contracting the virus and then disappear for years. Sometimes they linger and worsen, possibly resulting in death. Some people with HIV can go up to fifteen years or longer without serious complications. Most cases (95 to 100 percent) eventually develop into AIDS, for which there is no cure.

Treatment for HIV includes a number of *antibiotics* and *antiviral drugs* that prevent the virus from reproducing. The most common of these drugs is *AZT.* To prevent the spreading of HIV, infected and uninfected people should practice safe sex or *abstain* from sex altogether. Drug users are cautioned against reusing or sharing needles. Medical professionals commonly wear latex gloves when coming into contact with bodily fluids. HIV testing is common in order to determine whether or not an individual is infected.

Homegrown

A term for *marijuana* grown in a local area or in small quantities, usually for personal use. This form of marijuana may be stronger than normal because of selective breeding. Although it is illegal to grow, *possess*, or sell marijuana in the United States, it is estimated that 50 percent of the marijuana in this country is homegrown. It is often cheaper than marijuana that comes from other countries, mainly because the chain of drug *dealers* is shorter and fewer people take a cut of the profits. Many homegrown crops are hydroponically grown, or grown primarily in water/nutrient solutions without soil. These types of marijuana can be grown in closets, basements, and attics, making the plants easier to conceal.

Huffing

See *Volatile Solvent*.

Hydrocodone

A *synthetic opioid analgesic* similar to *codeine* and used as a pain reliever and a cough suppressant. Hydrocodone is commonly prescribed for back pain and migraine headaches and is often combined with *acetaminophen, aspirin,* or *ibuprofen*. This *drug* comes in pill form but is sometimes crushed and *snorted* by people who abuse it.

Like all *depressants,* hydrocodone slows the *central nervous system,* decreases *heart* rate, and slows respiration. In addition to relieving pain, hydrocodone may cause dizziness, sleepiness, nausea, vomiting, muscle spasms, constipation, difficulty in urinating, anxiety, mood swings, *depression,* rash, impaired mental abilities, and breathing difficulty. More serious *side effects* may include *cardiac arrhythmia* and unconsciousness. An *overdose* of this drug causes weakness, slow breathing, confusion, cold and clammy skin, *seizures, blackout, coma,* and death.

Hydrocodone has recently been the subject of controversy because more and more people are abusing it. It can lead to *physical* and *psychological dependence,* as well as *tolerance,* after only three to five days. *Withdrawal* symptoms are similar to those of codeine. Medical professionals advise against quitting this drug *cold turkey* because of the severity of the withdrawal symptoms.

Hypertension

High resting blood pressure. Most hypertension cases (essential hypertension) have no specific cause. Essential hypertension is not curable, but it is manageable. Approximately 10 percent of hypertension cases (secondary hypertension) are caused by *kidney* disease, hormonal disorders, certain *drugs* (particularly *cocaine*), obesity, stress, lack of exercise, excessive salt intake, *smoking tobacco,* and *alcoholism.*

Mild hypertension can go unnoticed for a long time. *Side effects* of mild hypertension may include headaches, dizziness, fatigue, and nosebleeds. When untreated for an extended time, hypertension can cause damage to the brain, eyes, *heart,* and kidneys. These symptoms manifest as fatigue, nausea, vomiting, difficulty in breathing, anxiety, confusion, and blurred vision. In the worst cases, hypertension can lead to *seizures, coma,* kidney failure, *stroke, heart failure, heart attack,* and death.

Treatment for mild hypertension includes weight loss and dieting. Patients should quit smoking and/or drinking, and also stop taking any potentially harmful drugs. In more severe cases, certain *prescription drugs* may be ordered, and the person may be admitted to a hospital for testing.

Blood pressure is measured with two values: Systolic pressure is the pressure when the heart contracts; diastolic pressure is the pressure when the heart relaxes. These values are represented with the systolic value first, the diastolic second, separated by a slash (e.g., 120/80). Blood pressure is measured in millimeters of mercury (ml Hg) because the earliest devices used mercury-filled tubes to measure blood pressure levels.

High blood pressure is normal for someone engaged in physical exertion. Hypertension occurs when a person is at rest. It can range from mild to severe, as outlined in the table below.

Resting Blood Pressure	Systolic (ml Hg)	Diastolic (ml Hg)
Low normal	Under 130	Under 85
High normal	130–139	85–89
Mild hypertension	140–159	90–99
Moderate hypertension	160–179	100–109
Extreme hypertension	180–209	110–119
Severe hypertension	210 and up	120 and up

Hypnotic-Sedative

Any *drug* that produces relaxation in small *doses* (sedative) and *intoxication* and sleep in larger doses (hypnotic). This group of drugs includes *barbiturates, benzodiazepines, tranquilizers, antianxiety drugs,* and *sleep aids.*

Hypnotic-sedatives are *central nervous system depressants,* and many of them are frequently prescribed for insomnia and anxiety disorders. The effects may include slurred speech, dizziness, nausea, vomiting, loss of coordination, slowed *heart* rate, slowed breathing, confusion, *euphoria,* mood swings, irritability, paranoia, and memory loss. A hypnotic-sedative *overdose,* or a mixture of these drugs and *alcohol,* can result in *blackout, coma,* and death.

Hypnotic-sedatives have a high potential for abuse. They can cause *physical* and *psychological dependence* and can lead to *tolerance.* Hypnotic-sedatives are abused by people who have trouble sleeping, by people with anxiety disorders, by *heroin* addicts (who mix them with heroin to increase the effects), and by others who enjoy the *high* these drugs give them.

Withdrawal symptoms related to hypnotic-sedatives can be quite severe, even life-threatening, and are similar to alcohol withdrawal. Symptoms of withdrawal include restlessness, anxiety, nausea, vomiting, insomnia, increased heart rate, sweating, tremors, muscle spasms, *hallucinations, seizures,* and death. Symptoms can last a week or longer; some individuals do not feel healthy for a month after quitting hypnotic-sedatives. The withdrawal symptoms related to barbiturate use are among the most severe. Many physicians advise not to quit these drugs *cold turkey,* but rather to cut back slowly.

Hypnotic-
Sedative

See also:
Delirium Tremens

I

- Ibuprofen
- Ice
- Immune System
  (effects of drugs on)
- Inhalant
- Inject
- Insulin
- Intervention
- Intoxication

Ibuprofen

An *analgesic* commonly found in *over-the-counter drugs* and pain relievers. Like *aspirin*, ibuprofen is a *nonsteroidal anti-inflammatory drug* (NSAID). Ibuprofen is primarily used to treat fever, headache, menstrual pain, and mild to moderate pain due to injury. Because it is an NSAID, ibuprofen also reduces swelling from burns, sprains, broken bones, and arthritis and similar conditions. Two *drugs* very similar to ibuprofen are ketoprofen and naproxen.

Negative *side effects* of ibuprofen may include cramps, indigestion, heartburn, diarrhea, and nausea. It may also cause ulcers. (Although it is very similar in nature to aspirin, ibuprofen may be somewhat gentler on the stomach.) Less common side effects may include dizziness, drowsiness, ringing in the ears, breathing difficulty, and fluid retention.

Persons who are allergic to aspirin may also be allergic to ibuprofen. An allergic reaction to ibuprofen may include rash, itching, and restriction of air passages. People who drink *alcohol* are at a greater risk of upset stomach, ulcers, and *liver* damage from taking ibuprofen.

Ice

A form of *methamphetamine* that is *smoked.* This *drug,* also called crystal meth, is made by dissolving methamphetamine in water and letting the water evaporate, leaving a white substance that looks like ice crystals. Ice is preferred by some drug users because it is more easily smoked than methamphetamine in powdered form. "Snot" is the term for a *freebase* form of ice.

Ice is often compared to *cocaine* and *crack,* but it is more dangerous because the effects last much longer, it is much cheaper, and it is powerfully addictive. Its effects are nearly the same as those of methamphetamine, but they set in more quickly and can last up to twenty-four hours. Ice causes intense *euphoria,* decreased appetite, and increased energy, often leading to fainting, insomnia, and nervous disorders. It can also cause *hypertension, cardiac arrhythmia,* shock, *seizures, coma,* and death.

Like methamphetamine, ice can quickly lead to *physical* and *psychological dependence.* When the drug wears off, the user can experience a *crash* as powerful as the *high,* involving profound *depression* and *withdrawal* symptoms.

Immune System (effects of drugs on)

The immune system is made up of many types of cells that protect the body from bacteria, viruses, parasites, and fungi that cause illnesses, as well as the development of *cancerous* tumors. In addition to cells, several organs also make up the immune system, including the thymus, spleen, bone marrow, and lymph nodes.

An immunodeficiency disorder is any of a large group of conditions characterized by a failure of the immune system, allowing infections and other diseases to occur more frequently and to last longer. An immunodeficiency disorder can cause fatal complications because it decreases the body's ability to protect itself from disease. Such disorders can be spread through the use of certain *drugs.* If *HIV*-positive users of illegal drugs (*heroin, methamphetamine,* and others) share their drug needles, they can spread the virus, which eventually develops into the fatal disease *AIDS*, or acquired immunodeficiency syndrome. Sharing needles can also result in chronic *hepatitis,* which can cause immuno-deficiency disorders. Some *alcohol*-related conditions may also cause immunodeficiency disorders, particularly *cirrhosis of the liver* and hepatitis. *Chemotherapy* may also cause diseases of the immune system.

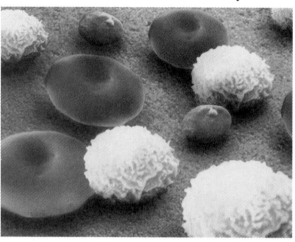

As part of the immune system, white blood cells protect the body from infections.

The prolonged use of many kinds of illegal drugs (and legal drugs like *tobacco* and alcohol) reduces the immune system's ability to fight infections and illnesses. Some drugs may cause an allergic reaction, which is essentially a hyperactive immune system. Other drugs are typically used to aid the immune system in fighting infections and sickness, particularly *antibiotics, antihistamines,* and anticancer drugs.

Drugs called immunosuppressants are used to purposely weaken the immune system during organ and tissue *transplants.* This is to counteract rejection, the body's natural reaction to the introduction of foreign materials.

Inhalant

Substance that produces *intoxicating* effects when its fumes are breathed in. Inhalants act as *depressants* on the *central nervous system*. These substances are absorbed by the tissues in the throat and *lungs* and carried rapidly to all parts of the body through the blood.

The *high* attained from inhalants is almost immediate and can last from a few seconds to a few hours depending on the substance. The short-term effects of inhalant abuse include lightheadedness, numbness, *hallucinations, euphoria,* distorted perception, floating sensations, numbness, *cardiac arrhythmia, blackout,* headache, spasms, and nausea. Long-term effects may include severe brain and central nervous system damage, *liver* and *kidney* damage, *cardiac arrest,* lung damage, *anemia,* and bone and bone marrow damage. Inhalants are commonly used by young people (twelve to sixteen) because they are legal and easy to find. Hundreds of products on the market are misused as inhalants. Inhalants can cause *psychological dependence.* Little or no *physical dependence* occurs, but they can create a *tolerance* in some users. Treatment for inhalant abuse most often entails calculating and managing organ damage and psychological counseling.

The various sources and effects of inhalants are outlined in the table below.

Inhalant	Chemical	Immediate Effects
Akyl nitrites	Amyl nitrite, Butyl nitrite	Euphoria, dizziness, sexual stimulation
Anesthetics	Ether	Pain relief, unconsciousness
	Nitrous oxide	Pain relief, intoxication, euphoria, hallucinations
Volatile Solvents (aerosols, glues/ adhesives, gases, cleaning solvents, etc.)	Toluene, ethyl acetate, hexane, methyl ethyl ketone, butane, propane, fluorocarbons, acetone, and many more	Lightheadedness, dizziness, intoxication, headache, hallucinations, cardiac arrhythmia, numbness, euphoria, weakness, spinning sensation, nausea, blackout

Inject

To put *drugs*—legal and illegal—into the body using a syringe. A syringe is a tube with a narrow nozzle fitted with a needle to penetrate the skin, and a rubber seal that can be depressed to inject drugs into the body or withdrawn to extract blood from the body. Injected drugs enter the bloodstream

Inject

See also:
Sudden Sniffing Death

more quickly than drugs taken in other manners, and as a result begin acting more quickly.

An intravenous injection goes directly into a vein, the quickest method of administering drugs. Drug users call this "mainlining." Injecting a drug into a muscle is called intramuscular injection. It involves a longer needle to reach the muscle and is used primarily when large amounts of a drug are needed. A subcutaneous injection is an injection beneath the skin, where the drug is absorbed by small blood vessels into the bloodstream.

Drug users who share needles to inject drugs are at risk of contracting viruses, particularly *hepatitis* and *HIV*. Repeated injections tend to cause open wounds that may become infected. The more often drugs are injected, the more difficult injections become because of the buildup of scar tissue. Habitual *heroin* users often have rows of scar tissue (or "needle tracks") up and down their arms and legs.

Insulin

A hormone secreted by the pancreas that prevents glucose (sugar) from building up in the bloodstream. With the aid of insulin, glucose is absorbed by the *liver* and by cells to be stored and used when the body needs extra energy.

When the pancreas produces little or no insulin—resulting in *hyperglycemia*—a person develops *diabetes mellitus*. Insulin is manufactured *synthetically* for people who have diabetes mellitus and who must *inject* it several times a day to keep their blood sugar at a safe level. Too much insulin can cause *hypoglycemia*, resulting in weakness, sweating, dizziness, and even *coma*. Diabetics are cautioned to carry a sugar source with them to counteract the effects of an insulin *overdose*. Synthetic insulin can also cause allergic reactions, including rash and breathing difficulty, but these reactions are rare.

Intervention

The process of confronting individuals with their self-destructive behavior—often the abuse of *drugs* and/or *alcohol*—and urging them to seek help to regain their physical and mental health. Often the first step of *drug rehabilitation*, interventions are usually organized by friends and family members of persons addicted to drugs, alcohol, or other self-destructive activity. The purpose is to help the individual recognize his or her problem by communicating about it in a straightforward, stern, yet compassionate manner.

Interventions can be highly successful, but they must be well organized. Plans should include a meeting of friends and family members to discuss the problem, who should be invited (the more caring people the better), what should be said, and where and when the intervention should be held. Some people make medical or counseling plans for the individual ahead of time. Poorly planned interventions can go awry, especially when the group has not planned what to say. Intervention groups usually have a leader or speaker. This person should not be confrontational, but compassionate and respectful.

This process is designed to prompt the individual to see his or her behavior as destructive and unhealthy, as well as a source of pain for the people close to him or her. While not always immediately successful, intervention often causes the individual to think hard about his or her actions and the effects they have on others.

Intoxication

See also:
Alcohol Poisoning

The effects of using *drugs* and *alcohol*. As the word suggests, intoxication involves the *toxic* results of introducing a *poison* into the body. Alcohol and most drugs are actually poisons.

Intoxication usually refers to the effects of alcohol consumption. *Blood alcohol level* is a measure of how much alcohol a person has in the bloodstream, or of how intoxicated he or she is. However, people react differently to alcohol consumption. Those who drink more often have higher alcohol *tolerance* levels. Generally speaking, the heavier a person is, the more alcohol it takes to produce intoxication. Studies have shown that some ethnic groups, such as those in Asian cultures, have lower alcohol tolerance levels and become intoxicated more quickly.

The effects of intoxication from drugs depend on the substance. *Depressants* such as alcohol and *barbiturates* cause slurred speech, loss of inhibitions, slowed breathing and *heart* rate, dizziness, nausea, vomiting, *blackout,* and even death if the *dose* is large enough. *Stimulants* such as *cocaine* and *methamphetamine* can cause accelerated heartbeat, increased energy, anxiety, mood swings, hyperactivity, and death. These and other poisons may cause *hallucinations, depression, seizures,* memory loss, *heart failure, cardiac arrhythmia, cardiac arrest,* and many other *side effects.* Although people may take drugs to relax or have a good time, they are still poisoning themselves and run the risk of permanent damage and death.

- Jaundice
- Joint

Jaundice

A yellow discoloration of the skin and eyes caused by abnormally high levels of a bile pigment called bilirubin in the blood. Bile is a yellowish fluid secreted by the *liver* into the intestines to aid in the digestion of fats. Bilirubin, produced by the breakdown of hemoglobin (the substance in red blood cells that carries oxygen), is actually a waste product found in bile and is normally excreted with bile into the intestines. When bilirubin excretion is impeded for any reason, it builds up in the blood, causing jaundice. Eliminated from the body through the *kidneys,* bilirubin gives urine a dark brown color.

Jaundice can occur from overproduction of bilirubin, the inability of bilirubin to pass from the liver cells into bile, or a blockage of the bile ducts flowing out of the liver. Conditions resulting in jaundice include *anemia,* damaged red blood cells, *hepatitis,* liver failure, gallstones or tumors in the bile ducts, and *cirrhosis of the liver.* Some newborns have jaundice caused by various conditions, including infection and blood type incompatibility with maternal blood.

Since jaundice is a sign of some greater problem, medical aid is usually needed to determine the cause. The individual may need surgical treatment, most often to remove bile duct blockage.

Joint

A *marijuana cigarette.* Joints are made by placing finely chopped marijuana on a thin piece of paper and rolling it into a cigarette. The ends of a joint are usually crimped or twisted to keep the *drug* from falling out. Joints are preferred by many drug users because they are less conspicuous than *pipes* and are sometimes mistaken for regular cigarettes.

A blunt is a larger type of joint made by cutting a cigar open, removing the *tobacco,* and replacing it with marijuana. These are preferred by some drug users because they last much longer and are more easily shared with a group.

Marijuana is often smoked by rolling it into a cigarette, or joint.

- Ketamine
- Kidneys (effects of drugs on)

Ketamine

An *anesthetic* used primarily by veterinarians, although it is sometimes used for humans, especially small children and the elderly. Ketamine is considered a "gentle" anesthetic that usually does not depress respiration. This *drug* comes in liquid and pill form. It can be *injected* or taken orally, but is sometimes crushed and *snorted*.

Ketamine is a strange drug that seems to defy categorization. It is considered a *hypnotic-sedative* that relieves pain by causing a "dissociative" feeling, meaning that it causes users to feel as if the mind is separated from the body. Users may feel as if events are not actually happening to them. Ketamine is chemically similar to *PCP* but is considered safer. Small *doses* lead to numbness, floating sensations, *euphoria*, nausea, vomiting, increased *heart* rate, and increased blood pressure, but ketamine usually does not affect respiration. In larger doses it leads to powerful *hallucinations* (more potent than *LSD*), out-of-body experiences, paranoid delusions, *blackout*, amnesia, depressed respiration, decreased heart rate and blood pressure, and possibly death. A ketamine *high* lasts for only about an hour. Ketamine can lead to *physical* and *psychological dependence* after only a week of use, and *tolerance* can develop in those who use it frequently.

While on ketamine, users may have no idea what is happening to them, which can result in accidents and injuries. Ketamine has also reportedly been abused as a *date-rape drug*.

Ketamine is a type of anesthetic that, when abused, can cause hallucinations and paranoia.

Kidneys

Kidneys (effects of drugs on)

The body has two kidneys, organs located below the *liver* and spleen near the back of the abdomen. The kidneys filter the blood and excrete waste products in the form of urine. *Drugs* and *alcohol* reach the liver via the bloodstream. The liver changes (or metabolizes) drugs and alcohol into substances that can easily be filtered out of the blood by the kidneys.

Certain drugs called diuretics cause the kidneys to remove more water from the blood than normal. These drugs are used to treat people who retain too much water in the body, or have suffered *heart failure* or certain kidney and liver disorders. Some drugs, such as *caffeine* and alcohol, have a diuretic effect.

Since the kidneys filter drugs from the body in the form of urine, prolonged or excessive drug use can cause kidney damage. Most kidney damage occurs in the tubules, tiny tubes through which blood passes. The tubules are where salts, water, and waste products are taken out of (and sometimes put back into) the blood. Renal failure (failure of the kidneys) can occur after taking excessive amounts of *analgesics* for a long time. A condition called nephrotic syndrome, caused by many diseases and certain drugs (such as *heroin* and analgesics), results in the loss of valuable proteins and the retention of high levels of salts, water, and fats in the blood. Certain *antibiotics* and anticancer drugs also can cause kidney problems. Someone with one or two dysfunctional kidneys (often a fatal condition) may need to have a kidney *transplant*. The donor is usually a close relative. A person can live with only one kidney.

- Laam
- "Laughing Gas"
- Laxative
- Legalization
- Librium
- Lidocaine
- Lithium
- Liver (effects of drugs on)
- Lorazepam
- Low Blood Pressure
- LSD
- Luminal
- Lungs (effects of drugs on)

Laam

Laam

Levo-alpha-acetyl-methadol is an *opioid analgesic* similar to *methadone*. Laam is a *maintenance drug* used by people addicted to *opiates* (particularly *heroin*) to prevent *relapse*. People who are prescribed laam must report to clinics to receive their regular *dose,* usually every two or three days. This schedule is designed to prevent abuse of laam, to avoid *overdose* (which can result in *coma* and death), and to avoid its being sold on the street as a heroin alternative.

In prescribed doses, laam relieves pain and depresses the *central nervous system* much as *morphine* does without causing *euphoria* or sedation. It also suppresses heroin *withdrawal* symptoms such as increased blood pressure, fever, tremors, cramps, nausea, vomiting, headache, weakness, and *craving* for heroin. *Side effects* of this drug, however, may include *low blood pressure,* dizziness, nausea, vomiting, diarrhea, and sweating (it is, after all, a *narcotic* similar to heroin). Laam can also lead to *physical* and *psychological dependence,* as well as *tolerance,* which is considered a positive side effect since it reduces the *high* received when the individual takes narcotic drugs, potentially making their use less appealing. Withdrawal from laam is similar to heroin, but it is less severe, sets in less quickly, and continues for a longer time.

Laam is a more recent maintenance drug than methadone and has certain advantages over it. Laam lasts longer than methadone, has fewer narcotic effects, and has less potential for abuse. Laam treatment can go on for years, allowing the user to go to work and carry on everyday activities such as driving a car.

"Laughing Gas"

See *Nitrous Oxide.*

Laxative

A *drug* that treats constipation (difficulty in eliminating feces). There are several kinds of laxatives. Some add bulk to feces, making it softer and easier to pass. Some stimulate intestinal contraction, expelling feces more quickly. Others increase the amount of salt in the feces, which in turn draws water into it, making it softer and easier to pass. Sometimes eating foods high in fiber and drinking large amounts of liquids will relieve constipation without the need for laxatives.

Negative *side effects* of laxative use include diarrhea, cramps, and improper vitamin absorption in the intestines. Some laxatives may cause *physical dependence* and should not be used for longer than a week. Constipation that lasts longer than a week may be a sign of a more serious problem, and the person should consult a doctor.

Legalization

See also:
Gateway Drug

A movement to end or modify legislation against *drug* distribution and *possession*. Some groups seek to make all drugs (both *hard* and *soft drugs*) legal to manufacture, sell, and use. Others are interested in a more con-trolled form of legalization, making some drugs legal, while others would remain controlled substances.

Groups in favor of legalization maintain that the "war on drugs" is unsuccessful and results in a waste of tax dollars. Many believe that the *medicinal use of illegal drugs* such as *marijuana* is reason enough to legalize them, or at least *decriminalize* them. Another argument highlights the potential increase in profits from the regulated production, sale, taxation, and advertisement of certain drugs. Others urge that if drugs were legalized, there would be more prison space for people who commit more violent *crimes*. Some even claim that legalization would reduce drug *addiction* rates simply by taking the mystery and thrill out of obtaining and using drugs.

Advocate for the legalization of marijuana and founder of the Cannabis Cultivators' Club, Dennis Peron.

Opponents of drug legalization declare that it would lead to an increase in addiction rates, crime, homelessness, the use of more harmful drugs, and child drug use. They declare that any money made from taxation of drugs would be spent on *drug rehabilitation* and similar social programs. They also argue that medicinal use of drugs like marijuana is unnecessary and that the prisons would be even more crowded because of violent crimes committed by drug users. Others point out the high number of health and social problems related to the consumption of *alcohol,* a legal drug.

Perhaps the most notable example of legalization is the situation in the Netherlands, where certain drugs (particularly marijuana and *hash*) are legally sold. Both sides of the legalization issue see this example in a different light. Proponents of legalization note that Holland's "harm reduction" legislation seeks to reduce the time and money wasted on the incarceration

Librium

See also:
Delirium Tremens

of people who buy and sell "soft drugs" comparable to alcohol and *tobacco*. They say it helps to differentiate between *recreational drug users* who pose no real risk to society, and those who represent a criminal element, mainly *dealers* and *traffickers* in hard drugs. Opponents of drug legalization point out that the Netherlands is considered the "drugstore of Europe," where soft and hard drug activities alike are ignored by officials. They claim that this has led to some of the highest addiction rates in the world, as well as high crime statistics.

Librium

The brand name of the *benzodiazepine* chlordiazepoxide prescribed to treat anxiety disorders and insomnia. It is also sometimes used to alleviate the symptoms of *alcohol withdrawal*. Librium can be taken orally or *injected*.

Like all *depressants*, Librium slows the *central nervous system*. It acts as a *hypnotic-sedative;* in small *doses* it causes sleepiness, and in larger doses it can cause unconsciousness. Negative *side effects* may include drowsiness, blurred vision, cramps, slurred speech, breathing difficulty, headache, clumsiness, mood swings, confusion, *cardiac arrhythmia,* trembling, *hallucinations,* and *seizures.* An *overdose* of Librium can result in weakness, tremors, lack of coordination, breathing difficulty, rash, bluish skin, drowsiness, *depression, intoxication,* confusion, anxiety, memory loss, *blackout, coma,* and death.

Taking Librium regularly for about two weeks can result in *physical* and *psychological dependence,* as well as *tolerance.* Withdrawal symptoms include cramps, muscle spasms, sweating, nausea, vomiting, insomnia, anxiety, tremors, and seizures. Medical professionals recommend against quitting Librium *cold turkey* because of the severity of the withdrawal symptoms, which can be similar to those of alcohol and *barbiturate* withdrawal.

Lidocaine

A local *anesthetic* used to numb body parts before minor surgery. It is also used to relieve pain of sunburn and hemorrhoids. Lidocaine is sometimes given intravenously after a *heart attack* to reduce the chance of *cardiac arrhythmia* and other complications. It can also be *injected* into the spine during childbirth to reduce pain. Lidocaine can be taken orally, injected, or applied to the skin as a lotion. Negative *side effects* of the drug may include nausea and vomiting.

Lithium

A metallic element of the periodic table, lithium has been used as a sedative and *antidepressant* for centuries. Lithium is similar to sodium and was actually used as a salt substitute in the early 1900s until it was found to cause deaths in *heart* patients. As a *drug* it is primarily used to treat patients with *mania* and bipolar disorder (mood swings between *depression* and mania). Since it is more effective on manic disorders, lithium is sometimes mixed with antidepressants (such as *Prozac*) to treat manic-depressive disorder. Lithium, however, is known to stop acting for patients with more persistent cases of mania and depression. Lithium is taken orally and may take one to three weeks to affect the patient.

Lithium typically acts as a mild *tranquilizer* and acts to reduce excess nerve activity by balancing the levels of neurotransmitters (chemical messengers) in the *central nervous system*. Negative *side effects* include diarrhea, frequent urination, rash, nausea, vomiting, and tremors. Less common side effects may include acne, blurred vision, anxiety, drowsiness, stupor, difficulty in concentrating, mood swings, bluish skin, trouble sleeping, *low blood pressure, cardiac arrhythmia, kidney* damage, *seizures, blackout, coma,* and death. Lithium can cause a patient to lose too much salt, leading to dehydration, dizziness, and fainting. Long-term use of lithium can result in thyroid problems, including goiter, and can worsen certain kidney problems. People with thyroid disorders, heart problems or kidney problems, or *diabetes* should avoid using lithium.

Lithium is not believed to be habit forming and has no *withdrawal* symptoms. A lithium *overdose* can result in slurred speech, weakness, lack of coordination, seizures, trouble in urinating, thirst, rash, diarrhea, nausea, vomiting, low blood pressure, cardiac arrhythmia, fatigue, coma, and death.

Liver (effects of drugs on)

The liver is an organ below the *lungs* on the right side of the body that metabolizes the nutrients and vitamins in foods and beverages. It changes nutrients into chemicals the body can use to aid growth and preserve health. In addition, the liver detoxifies, or cleanses, the blood of *poisonous* substances, eliminating them through the *kidneys.*

Many poisonous substances (including *drugs* and *alcohol*) are processed in the liver. Drugs and alcohol can become even more *toxic* when acted upon by the liver. People who frequently consume poisonous substances run the risk of developing liver diseases such as *cancer, cirrhosis,* tumors, *hepatitis,* and others.

Liver

See also:
Antipsychotic Drug
Hypnotic-Sedative

Perhaps the most damaging substance for the liver is alcohol. People who abuse alcohol (or even use it regularly) can suffer permanent liver damage, including fat accumulation in the liver, inflammation of the liver (hepatitis), and scarring of the liver (cirrhosis). A damaged liver is less able to rid the body of harmful substances. This may result in a hepatic *coma*, a potentially fatal condition characterized by sleepiness, confusion, stupor, and hand tremors. When the liver becomes irreparably damaged by alcohol (or other poisons), it may be necessary to perform a liver *transplant* to save the life of the patient.

Lorazepam

See also:
Antianxiety Drug
Hypnotic-Sedative

A *benzodiazepine* that acts as a *tranquilizer* as well as a sedative. Lorazepam is most often prescribed for anxiety disorders and *depression* but is sometimes used as a presurgery *anesthetic*. It is also prescribed to help control epileptic *seizures*. The *drug* is taken orally or *injected*.

Like most *depressants*, lorazepam slows the *central nervous system*, but in moderate *doses* it usually does not affect breathing and *heart* rate. Negative *side effects* may occur upon initially taking this drug but commonly disappear after continued use or after reducing the dosage. These side effects may include sleepiness, weakness, lack of coordination, nausea, vomiting, headache, rash, *depression, low blood pressure,* and memory loss. Lorazepam injections have been known to cause *hypertension,* low blood pressure, rash, nausea, vomiting, and short-term memory loss. An *overdose* of lorazepam can cause sleepiness, confusion, low blood pressure, depressed respiration, *blackout, coma,* and death.

Lorazepam can cause *physical* and *psychological dependence,* as well as *tolerance. Withdrawal* symptoms are similar to those of *alcohol* and *barbiturate* withdrawal: sweating, insomnia, cramps, nausea, vomiting, tremors, and seizures. The severity depends on duration of use and size of doses.

Low Blood Pressure

See also:
Hypertension

Also called hypotension, low blood pressure occurs most commonly from standing up too quickly, but it can also be caused by injuries involving blood loss, *diabetes*, shock, *heart attack*, large *doses* of certain *drugs*, and *alcohol*. Low blood pressure can cause dizziness and *blackout* from lack of oxygen reaching the brain.

Some people naturally have low blood pressure, and it is not always a cause for alarm. Younger people normally have low blood pressure; the older people get, the higher their blood pressure usually rises. People with blood pressure lower than normal live longer on average than those with normal or high blood pressure. Treating chronic or problematic low blood pressure is a matter of treating the underlying cause.

LSD

Lysergic acid diethylamide is a *hallucinogenic drug* manufactured from *ergot*. LSD is a liquid that is dropped on the tongue, applied to small squares of paper or sugar cubes to be eaten, or added to drinks. The drug begins acting thirty to ninety minutes after consumption and can last up to twelve hours. A few drops are very potent.

The effects of LSD are unpredictable. An LSD *high,* called a *trip,* can cause dilated pupils, increased *heart* rate, increased blood pressure, increased energy, sweating, loss of appetite, insomnia, dry mouth, tremors, unpredictable mood swings, *depression,* paranoid delusions, and *hallucinations.* Although LSD use does not cause death directly, it can lead to death indirectly, particularly from accidents and delusion-generated injuries.

Some users, especially inexperienced ones, undergo particularly "bad trips" because they are not prepared for the intensity of the effects of LSD; even experienced users can have bad trips, which may involve intense paranoia, depression, fear, frightening hallucinations, and panic attacks. The best remedy for a bad trip is a quiet room and the company of a friend.

LSD is not addictive, and most people quit using it after a short period of *experimentation* or a longer period of habitual use. LSD use can lead to *tolerance* in as little as three days, but users do not usually suffer *withdrawal* symptoms. People who use this drug may experience *flashbacks* weeks, months, or years after they stop using it.

LSD is considered a *recreational drug* and is most often taken in social circles and large groups. It is widely used as a *club drug* and is often found at concerts and raves (all-night dances).

Luminal

The brand name of the *barbiturate* phenobarbital, a *hypnotic-sedative* used to treat insomnia and anxiety. Luminal is also used to prevent *seizures* in people who have epilepsy and to treat a seizure in progress. The *drug* is taken orally or *injected.*

Like all *depressants,* Luminal slows the *central nervous system.* Negative *side effects* may include sleepiness, poor coordination, *intoxication,* dizziness, nausea, vomiting, headache, nightmares, nervousness, fever, swollen face and tongue, breathing difficulty, hives, easy bruising or bleeding, burning at

injection site, *low blood pressure,* decreased *heart* rate, decreased breathing, *cardiac arrhythmia, hallucinations,* difficulty in concentrating, confusion, and *anemia.* Long-term use can lead to *liver* damage. An overdose of Luminal results in slowed or halted breathing, slow heart beat, low blood pressure, headache, *heart failure, pneumonia,* confusion, delirium, *blackout,* deep sleep, *coma,* and death.

Luminal can lead to *physical* and *psychological dependence* in just two weeks. Prolonged use can lead to *tolerance,* sometimes causing the user to take larger *doses,* which can result in *overdose. Withdrawal* symptoms include anxiety, muscle spasms, tremors, fatigue, dizziness, nausea, vomiting, insomnia, hallucinations, delirium, seizures, and death.

Lungs (effects of drugs on)

Different *drugs* have a variety of negative *side effects* on the lungs. *Depressants* such as *hypnotic-sedatives, tranquilizers, alcohol, barbiturates, benzodiazepines,* and *narcotics* can slow the rate of respiration and make breathing difficult. In high *doses,* these drugs can cause *blackout* from a lack of oxygen reaching the brain and halted respiration. At the other end of the spectrum, *stimulants* like *amphetamines, cocaine, MDMA,* and *herbal stimulants* can increase respiration, which is usually less dangerous than depressed respiration.

The number one cause of lung *cancer* is *smoking tobacco. Cigarettes* and other tobacco products cause the buildup of tar and other harmful chemicals in the lungs, including about forty *carcinogens.* Other lung diseases caused by cigarette smoke include chronic *bronchitis, pneumonia, emphysema,* and asthma. Even *secondhand smoke* can cause these ailments when a person is subjected to it for an extended period of time. Long-term *marijuana* use is believed to have the same effects on the lungs.

Inhalant abuse can result in burned lung tissue or lung tissue that becomes coated with the inhaled substance, causing death from a lack of oxygen reaching the brain. In fact, any inhaled drug can have this effect on the body, since it naturally takes the place of oxygen entering the lungs. People who abuse narcotics, especially *heroin,* can develop lung problems like pneumonia, pulmonary embolism (blood clot in an artery of the lung), and abscesses in the lungs.

M

- "Magic Mushroom"
- Mainline
- Maintenance Drug
- Mania
- Marijuana
- MDMA
- Medicinal Uses of Illegal Drugs
- Meprobamate
- Mescaline
- Methadone
- Methamphetamine
- Monoamine Oxidase
  Inhibitor (MAOI)
- Morphine
- Motion Sickness Drug

"Magic Mushroom"

See *Psilocybin.*

Mainline

See *Inject.*

Maintenance Drug

Prescription drug that helps a person maintain *sobriety,* particularly one that blocks *heroin cravings* and reduces the potential for *relapse.* Alcoholics are sometimes prescribed *drugs* when trying to quit drinking *alcohol.* Maintenance drugs may also be considered *antidotes* because they counteract the effects of more harmful substances. This method of treatment is often combined with other methods, such as *twelve-step programs* and counseling.

Mania

A mental disorder characterized by excessive activity, *euphoria,* and anxiety for no apparent reason. Mania usually manifests as a symptom of bipolar disorder, a condition distinguished by extreme mood swings, from mania to *depression.* Most manic episodes last from a week to a few months and often result in depression.

People who develop mania are usually happier and more active than normal at first. This may make mania difficult to diagnose initially. However, happiness may give way to irritability and even aggression. As the disorder develops, the person may display frequent impatience, increased activity, lack of sleep or interest in sleep, difficulty in concentrating, and violent outbursts. He or she may have delusions of persecution and see and hear things that are not really present. Mania can also lead to *addiction* to *drugs, alcohol,* gambling, and even sex. If the disorder is allowed to progress, it can lead to delusions of power, wealth, and intellect; people with mania sometimes even believe they are God.

Treatment for mania is usually based on *prescription antianxiety drugs. Lithium* is particularly helpful in treating mania, but it takes one to two weeks to act. Some *benzodiazepines* are also helpful in treating mania, especially *lorazepam.* Lithium is used in cases of bipolar disorder. Formerly known as manic-depressive disorder, bipolar disorder involves recurring onsets of mania and depression. Lithium lessens the mood swings between mania and depression. In rare cases, people with mania are admitted to a hospital for observation.

Marijuana

Marijuana

The leaves, seeds, stems, and buds (flowers) of the hemp plant (*Cannabis sativa*). Users most often inhale the smoke produced from burning this *drug*—either as a *joint* or in a *pipe*—but it can also be ingested. Marijuana produces lightheadedness or a *high* in its users. Although it contains more than 400 chemicals, only one is responsible for the feeling of lightheadedness—tetrahydrocannabinol, or *THC*.

Short-term effects of *smoking* marijuana include increased *heart* rate, loss of coordination, distorted perception, anxiety, and *depression*. A marijuana high lasts two to three hours, but the negative effects can last up to two days. Some long-term effects are similar to those of smoking *tobacco:* deterioration of *lung* tissue, chronic *bronchitis,* and frequent chest colds. THC suppresses the neurons in the information-processing system in an area of the brain called the hippocampus, and some researchers believe that heavy marijuana use can result in permanent brain damage.

Marijuana is considered a *recreational drug,* one that is usually shared with others in social surroundings. For some, smoking marijuana can become habitual.

Addiction to marijuana is primarily a psychological problem, not a physical one. *Withdrawal* symptoms do not occur when the drug is discontinued, but some extreme users report interrupted sleep and edginess when they quit. Treatment possibilities include outpatient and residential programs, often in conjunction with *twelve-step programs.* Other types of treatment include home or family-based treatment for youths, group counseling, and individual counseling.

The hemp plant can be easily identified by the shape of its leaves.

MDMA

MDMA, or 3, 4-methylenedioxymethamphetamine, is a *stimulant* commonly known as ecstasy. It is chemically similar to *methamphetamine* and is a *hallucinogen* similar to *mescaline*. It is a derivative of a similar *drug* called MDA, or methylenedimethoxyamphetamine. MDMA affects the way a neurotransmitter (chemical messenger) called *serotonin* acts in the *central nervous system*. The drug comes in powder or pill form and can be swallowed, *snorted*, or *injected*. The effects begin in thirty minutes and last four to six hours.

MDMA was originally manufactured in 1913 as a *diet drug* but was quickly found to be unpredictable and disappeared for decades. MDMA, MDA, and similar drugs reappeared in the 1960s and quickly became known as "love drugs" because they typically enhance a person's sense of compassion. Other *side effects* of MDMA include increased *heart* rate, hyperactivity, increased confidence, increased body heat, increased sexual impulses, *euphoria, hallucinations,* dehydration, nervousness, muscular tension, and talkativeness. More serious effects may include anxiety, paranoia, and *cardiac arrhythmia.* An MDMA *overdose* results in high blood pressure, insomnia, panic attacks, heat stroke, *heart failure, seizures, blackout,* and death. Recent research has revealed that long-term MDMA use causes *depression,* memory loss, and brain damage.

Ecstasy is commonly found in pill form.

MDMA can lead to *psychological dependence* and *tolerance*. It is still unclear if it causes *physical dependence* and *withdrawal* symptoms. Although it is often manufactured in underground labs, MDMA is not a *designer drug* (because it is listed as a controlled substance). It is considered a *club drug* because of its hallucinogenic properties and the extra energy it gives its users, and because it makes users especially friendly. MDMA sometimes causes death when a user dances for hours in a hot club and becomes dehydrated to the point of exhaustion and heart failure.

Medicinal Uses of Illegal Drugs

See also:
Decriminalization
Legalization

Many illegal *drugs* were first developed to be used as medicinal drugs but were found to be unsafe and were labeled controlled, illegal substances. *Cocaine* was considered an effective *anesthetic* and *analgesic* until it was replaced by safer, less addictive drugs. *Opioid analgesics* similar to *heroin*

(like *morphine* and *codeine*) are still used as powerful pain relievers and cough suppressants, but they are highly regulated because of their addictive qualities. *Rohypnol* is a powerful *hypnotic-sedative* that is illegal in the United States but is legally sold in Mexico, South America, and Europe. The drugs *PCP*, *methamphetamine*, and *LSD* were originally developed for legitimate purposes but were deemed unsafe and illegal after extensive testing.

The use of *marijuana* and *synthetic* cannabis derivatives is currently a widely debated topic. Marijuana has been found to be an effective treatment for a number of ailments and diseases. It has been used to treat the *side effects* of *cancer* treatment, *AIDS*, multiple sclerosis, and other diseases that cause chronic pain, tremors, nausea, and loss of appetite. Marijuana decreases ocular pressure in people who have glaucoma and can sometimes cure patients of this condition. Chronic *seizures* (epilepsy) have been treated with marijuana, although it is not successful in all patients. The drug is also helpful in treating nausea and loss of appetite, the negative side effects of *chemotherapy*.

See also:
Hypertension

Meprobamate

An *antianxiety drug* used to treat anxiety, tension, and muscle spasms. Meprobamate is a *tranquilizer* similar in effect (but not composition) to *barbiturates*, but not as potent. This *drug* is combined with *aspirin* to treat moderate pain and anxiety and is sometimes used before surgery. It is rarely used as a *sleep aid*. Meprobamate comes in pill form and is used less frequently today.

Like most *depressants*, meprobamate slows down the *central nervous system*. *Side effects* include dizziness, irritability, fatigue, confusion, weakness, headache, slurred speech, blurred vision, rash, diarrhea, nausea, vomiting, confusion, and *euphoria*. More serious effects may include fever, swollen ankles, slow heartbeat, *cardiac arrhythmia*, breathing difficulty, numbness, bruising, and *blackout*. Meprobamate *overdose* causes weakness, blurred vision, bluish skin, nausea, vomiting, tremors, extreme confusion, breathing difficulty, *seizures, blackout, coma*, and death.

People who take large *doses* of meprobamate to achieve a *high* may experience slurred speech, euphoria, and dizziness. Meprobamate can lead to *physical* and *psychological dependence*. Users can develop *tolerance* to it and experience *withdrawal* symptoms when they quit after long-term use. Withdrawal symptoms are similar to those of *alcohol* and *barbiturates*, and may include tremors, confusion, *hallucinations*, and seizures.

Mescaline

Mescaline

A *hallucinogen* found in cactus plants—most notably peyote—that grow in the southwestern United States and northern Mexico. Peyote itself contains some fifty psychoactive ingredients (chemicals that affect the mind), including mescaline. Mescaline was one of the first hallucinogens to be *synthetically* manufactured in labs. It takes about an hour to affect the user and lasts about twelve hours. Mescaline is usually taken orally in the form of peyote "buttons" (dried top parts of the cactus plants), but it can also be made into a powder and put into capsules, *smoked,* and even *injected.*

Mescaline produces effects similar to *amphetamines* by increasing blood pressure, heartbeat, body temperature, and respiration. It is also similar to *LSD* (although far less potent) in that it causes *hallucinations* by altering the levels of certain neurotransmitters (chemical messengers) in the *central nervous system.* Other *side effects* include itching, vomiting (most often from its offensive taste), lack of coordination, mood swings, feelings of empathy with others, and subjectively spiritual experiences. A mescaline *overdose* may result in paranoid delusions, "bad *trip*" (an unpleasant hallucinogen *high*), confusion, and possibly death.

Mescaline does not cause *physical dependence,* but it may cause *psychological dependence,* as well as *tolerance.* No *withdrawal* symptoms occur. While it is illegal for most people to possess mescaline, members of certain Native American religious groups may possess it for religious practices. These groups have been using peyote and similar hallucinogenic substances for hundreds of years. The hallucinations are considered spiritual visions.

Methadone

Methadone is administered orally to people who are breaking an addiction to heroin or other opiates.

An *opioid analgesic* used by people trying to break addiction to *opiates* (particularly *heroin*) to help prevent *relapse.* This use is as a *maintenance drug,* but methadone is also used in larger *doses* as a pain reliever after surgery. People who are prescribed methadone must report to clinics to receive their regular dose every day (although in rare cases individuals are given a take-home supply). This schedule is designed to prevent methadone abuse, to avoid *overdose* (which can result in *coma* and death), and to avoid it being sold on the street as a heroin alternative.

Methadone relieves pain and depresses the *central nervous system* as *morphine* does without causing *euphoria* or sedation (in prescribed doses). It also suppresses the heroin *withdrawal* symptoms of increased blood pressure, fever, tremors, cramps, nausea, vomiting, headache, weakness, and *craving* for heroin. *Side effects*, however, may include *low blood pressure*, dizziness, nausea, vomiting, and sweating (it is, after all, a *narcotic* similar to heroin). Methadone can also lead to *physical* and *psychological dependence*, as well as *tolerance*, which is considered a positive side effect since it reduces the *high* obtained when the individual takes narcotic drugs, potentially making narcotic use less appealing. Withdrawal from methadone is also similar to that of heroin, but it is less severe, sets in less quickly, and continues longer.

Methadone treatment can be an ongoing process, sometimes lasting up to ten years. People can function safely on methadone, and it is possible to drive a car and work at a job while on this drug. Critics say that methadone treatment is replacing one *addiction* with another, but others praise it for its ability to help heroin addicts lead normal lives.

Methamphetamine

An illegal *synthetic amphetamine*. This *drug* is a powerful *stimulant* that speeds up the *central nervous system* similar to the way *adrenaline* does. The effects last eight to twenty-four hours, depending on the form and *dosage*. Methamphetamine is made in underground labs from *over-the-counter drugs* (*ephedrine*, for example) and other ingredients (hydrochloric acid, battery acid, lye, antifreeze) that are easy to obtain. It can be taken orally, *smoked*, *snorted*, or *injected*.

Side effects of this drug include increased alertness, itching, numbness, increased heartbeat, loss of appetite, talkativeness, nervousness, mood swings, insomnia, confusion, aggressive behavior, false sense of power, *hallucinations*, muscle spasms, and *depression*. More serious effects may include *cardiac arrhythmia*, extreme rise in body temperature, *seizures*, and *blackout*. A methamphetamine *overdose* results in high fever, seizures, *heart failure*, *stroke*, and death. The effects of long-term methamphetamine use include blood vessel damage, brain damage, schizophrenia, chronic hallucinations, *kidney* damage, *liver* damage, *lung* problems, chronic depression, malnutrition, damaged *immune system*, and paranoid delusions.

Methamphetamine use can lead to *physical* and *psychological dependence*. *Withdrawal* symptoms include extreme depression, anxiety, fatigue, paranoia, aggressive behavior, and hunger. A methamphetamine *high* can be very exhilarating and can kick in very quickly (often called a "rush"). When

it wears off, however, users experience a profound *crash,* and they usually *crave* more of the drug to avoid depression and withdrawal symptoms. This situation often leads to methamphetamine *relapse* during *drug rehabilitation.*

Methamphetamine is taken for the intense sense of *euphoria* it gives its users and its ability to increase physical stamina. It is often abused as a *club drug* for these reasons.

Monoamine Oxidase Inhibitor (MAOI)

A class of *antidepressants* used to treat *depression.* MAOIs raise the levels of certain neurotransmitters (chemical messengers) in the brain that naturally fight depression and other mental illnesses. It commonly takes two to three weeks for the positive effects of MAOIs to set in.

In addition to raising the levels of neurotransmitters in the brain, MAOIs also keep the body from metabolizing certain compounds, thus making some foods *toxic.* People taking MAOIs for depression are placed on a restrictive diet that avoids a long list of foods, including aged cheeses and meats, chicken liver, certain types of beans, salted fish, chocolate, beer, yogurt, sour cream, over-ripe fruits, monosodium glutamate, soy sauce, meat tenderizers, and others. These foods can cause hypertensive crisis, a very dangerous and rapid form of *hypertension.* People taking MAOIs are also instructed to carry an MAOI *antidote* in case of emergency.

MAOIs are used when other antidepressants have failed because they are more dangerous and unpredictable. Short-term *side effects* include *cardiac arrhythmia,* dizziness, insomnia, weight gain, excessive sweating, constipation, muscle cramps, and sexual dysfunction. Unlike other antidepressants, MAOIs do not lead to sedation as often. MAOIs can have negative and fatal reactions when mixed with other medications, especially other antidepressants.

Tolerance and *addiction* to MAOIs are rare. Most problems occur when the patient fails to take a large enough *dose* or abruptly stops using MAOIs. At this point *withdrawal* symptoms may occur, including nausea, vomiting, cramps, diarrhea, chills, insomnia, and anxiety.

Morphine

A quick-acting *opioid analgesic* used to treat moderate to severe pain due to *heart attack*, serious injury, surgery, and *cancer*. This drug also typically makes patients feel carefree as it makes pain less bothersome. Morphine is usually given only as a last resort because it is a strong *depressant* that can slow breathing and heartbeat. It can be taken orally or *injected*. It also comes in powder form, which is sometimes *snorted* by abusers.

In addition to pain relief, short-term *side effects* of morphine include fatigue, dry mouth, weakness, *euphoria*, constipation, rash, itching, headache, dizziness, blurred vision, sweating, nausea, vomiting, difficulty in concentrating, and confusion. More serious effects may include *hallucinations*, tremors, *low blood pressure*, *cardiac arrhythmia*, breathing difficulty, *blackout*, *coma*, and death. A morphine *overdose* can result in muscle spasms, breathing difficulty, bluish skin, stomach cramps, confusion, low blood pressure, cardiac arrhythmia, blackout, *seizures*, coma, and death. Long-term effects may include malnutrition, impaired *immune system*, and infection of the *heart* valves.

Morphine use can lead to *physical* and *psychological dependence*, as well as *tolerance*. *Withdrawal* symptoms are the same as those of *heroin* abuse and include nausea, vomiting, sweating, cramps, and tremors. People experiencing chronic pain due to injury or cancer can quickly form an *addiction* to morphine. Treatment for addiction often includes *maintenance drugs* such as *methadone* or *laam*.

Motion Sickness Drug

Antihistamines—prescription and *over-the-counter drugs*—that help prevent nausea, vomiting, and related sicknesses while traveling in cars, planes, and boats. These *drugs* work best when taken thirty minutes to an hour before traveling. Since antihistamines cause sleepiness, people who plan on driving a motor vehicle (or any other vehicle) should not use them. Negative *side effects* are rare but may include blurred vision, headache, cramps, constipation, and *cardiac arrhythmia*.

- Naltrexone
- Narcotic
- Narcotics Anonymous
- Needle Tracks
- Nembutal
- Nicotine
- Nightshade
- Nitrous Oxide
- Nonsteroidal
  Anti-inflammatory Drug
- Novocaine

Naltrexone

A *prescription drug* used to treat *narcotic addiction* and *alcoholism*. Naltrexone blocks narcotic and *alcohol cravings,* as well as their pleasurable effects. It comes in pill form, and a single *dose* lasts for twenty-four hours.

Naltrexone binds to *opioid receptors* in the brain, blocking the *high* from narcotics and alcohol, thus blocking the pleasure in using them. Additional *side effects* may include rash, dizziness, nausea, vomiting, headache, insomnia, cramps, chills, constipation, diarrhea, blurred vision, confusion, anxiety, loss of appetite, fever, *hallucinations, depression,* mood changes, breathing difficulty, and *cardiac arrhythmia.* Most of these symptoms are rare and should disappear shortly after beginning treatment. In excess doses, naltrexone can cause *liver* damage.

Naltrexone should not be considered a cure for alcoholism or addiction to narcotic *drugs.* It can help overcome these addictions when it is part of a *drug rehabilitation* program including counseling and *twelve-step programs.* Naltrexone treatment should begin only after the person is no longer dependent on narcotics or alcohol because it can trigger *withdrawal* symptoms. Efforts to cancel out the effects of this drug by taking narcotics can result in *coma* or death. Naltrexone does not block the impairment caused by consuming alcohol, just the *euphoric* effects (in other words, it won't "*sober* you up"). Since naltrexone does not induce a high, it is not addictive. It has no withdrawal symptoms.

Narcotic

An addictive *drug*—primarily an *opiate*—used to treat pain. The term *"opioid analgesic"* refers to narcotics medically used to treat moderate to severe pain, such as *codeine* and *morphine.* Some narcotics, such as *heroin,* are illegal and have little or no medicinal significance. Some are naturally derived from the poppy plant, while others are *synthetically* manufactured, as with *fentanyl.* These drugs can be taken orally, *smoked,* or *injected.*

Narcotics are *depressants,* which slow the *central nervous system,* causing *low blood pressure,* decreased *heart* rate, depressed breathing, and fatigue. Other *side effects* include pain relief, *euphoria,* constipation, flushed skin, itching, low body temperature, and a lack of concern for events happening around the user. An *overdose* of narcotics can result in slowed breathing, fluid in the *lungs, seizures, blackout, coma,* and death.

Opiates are used throughout the world, often smoked in "opium dens." Here, two men smoke opium from a pipe and a bong in an opium den in Thailand.

Narcotics
Anonymous

See also:
Maintenance Drug
Opiate/Opium

Long-term effects of narcotic abuse can include lung problems, impaired *immune system,* and brain damage. The use of needles to inject narcotics can result in *hepatitis* and *HIV* (from sharing infected needles), skin infections, scar tissue on the arms and legs, and lymph node infections.

Some people abuse narcotics because of chronic pain; others use illegal and *prescription* narcotics for their euphoric effects. Narcotics can lead to *physical* and *psychological dependence* in as little as two days, and users quickly build a *tolerance. Withdrawal* from narcotics can be quite severe but is not life-threatening. Withdrawal symptoms include anxiety, increased heartbeat, rapid breathing, sweating, goosebumps, tremors, nausea, vomiting, aching muscles, and diarrhea. These symptoms usually occur four to six hours after last using the drug and can last up to two weeks or more. Treatment for narcotic *addiction* may include *detoxification, maintenance drugs,* counseling, and *twelve-step programs (Narcotics Anonymous).*

Narcotics Anonymous

See *Twelve-Step Program.*

Needle Tracks

See *Inject.*

Nembutal

The brand name of the *barbiturate* phenobarbital, which is used to treat and prevent *seizures.* This *drug* is also used to treat insomnia, anxiety, and high blood pressure.

Like all *depressants,* Nembutal slows the *central nervous system,* resulting in decreased blood pressure, depressed respiration, and slowed heartbeat. Other *side effects* may include blurred vision, slurred speech, slowed reflexes, drowsiness, dizziness, irritability, confusion, anxiety, headache, and nightmares. Less common but more severe effects may include allergic reaction, closing of the throat, itching, swollen lips, fever, and bruising. An *overdose* of Nembutal can result in *kidney* failure, breathing difficulty, *pneumonia,* weak pulse, *low blood pressure, heart attack,* delirium, *blackout, coma,* and death. Long-term effects may include *anemia, liver* damage, and *depression.*

Nembutal can cause *physical* and *psychological dependence,* as well as *tolerance. Withdrawal* symptoms include restlessness, anxiety, insomnia, sweating, and fever. Doctors advise against quitting Nembutal *cold turkey* because the withdrawal symptoms can be quite severe. It is better to cut back gradually.

Nicotine

The *drug* found in *tobacco* to which people become addicted. Nicotine is a *stimulant* found in tobacco plants, but it can also be *synthetically* manufactured. When tobacco is *smoked* or chewed, nicotine enters the bloodstream and speeds up the *central nervous system* in about eight seconds. Some derivatives of nicotine are used as strong pesticides.

Nicotine is actually a powerful *poison;* as little as two drops could be fatal. Most *cigarettes* contain approximately one milligram of nicotine. New smokers must build a *tolerance* for nicotine before the *toxic* symptoms pass. These symptoms (sometimes called nicotine *intoxication*) include vertigo, rapid/slow heartbeat, headache, nausea, vomiting, and sometimes *blackout*. For people who have built a tolerance to nicotine, the *side effects* of smoking include increased heartbeat, narrowed blood vessels, high blood pressure, extra alertness, and an energy boost. Excessive nicotine intake can result in vomiting, *seizures*, and (rarely) death. Nicotine causes some people to use tobacco products for many years and is subsequently the main cause of many long-term problems, including coronary *heart* disease, *hypertension*, *cancer*, peptic ulcers (sores in the lining of the stomach), and disorders of the reproductive system.

Nicotine is one of the most widely used drugs in the world and one of the most addictive. Some researchers believe it is as addictive as *heroin*, *barbiturates*, and *alcohol*, or more so. Nicotine can lead to *physical* and *psychological dependence*, as well as tolerance. *Withdrawal* symptoms may include drowsiness, fatigue, headaches, nausea, vomiting, insomnia, hand tremors, sweating, difficulty in concentrating, irritability, anxiety, and even seizures. Nicotine withdrawal can be quite difficult to manage, and *relapse* often occurs.

Nightshade

A large group of plants that contain a *poisonous* substance called solanine. Many common plants and vegetables are members of the nightshade family, including tomatoes, potatoes, eggplants, and certain peppers. The levels of solanine in these vegetables are so low that they are harmless. *Tobacco* is also a member of the nightshade family.

Some nightshade plants are used to make certain *prescription drugs*, particularly sedatives. These same plants also have a history of being abused for their *euphoric* effects. Belladonna (Italian for "beautiful lady") was once used as a cosmetic by women to dilate the eyes. It can be found in sedatives, muscle relaxants, asthma medications, and *anesthetics*. Belladonna is

Nightshade

See also:
Cigarette/Cigar

See also:
Hypnotic-Sedative

sometimes used to treat eye diseases, stomach cramps and pain, and *cardiac arrhythmia,* and is believed to be an *antidote* to *opium*-based *drugs.* This drug increases *heart* rate. Belladonna was abused in medieval times as a *hallucinogen.* Similar to belladonna is a plant called jimsonweed.

The *side effects* of nightshade include low body temperature, fever, slowed breathing, cramps, nausea, vomiting, diarrhea, slow or rapid pulse, lack of coordination, weakness, headache, delirium, *hallucinations,* shock, and paralysis. Although rare, a nightshade *overdose* can result in *seizures, blackout, coma,* and death.

Nitrous Oxide

See also:
Sudden Sniffing Death

A colorless, odorless gas used as an *anesthetic* by physicians and dentists because it temporarily eliminates pain. Nitrous oxide is also known as "laughing gas" because people become *euphoric* and silly when inhaling it. Even though it is considered a weak anesthetic, unconsciousness can result if enough is inhaled.

Nitrous oxide is frequently abused as an *inhalant.* Used as a propellant in *aerosol* products, nitrous oxide, or "whip-its," could once be obtained easily by young children and teens. In the past few years stores have instituted precautions, such as keeping certain products in a locked cabinet, to prevent their abuse.

Several dangers are associated with this anesthetic when abused as an inhalant:

1. Nitrous oxide can cause disorientation that sometimes results in physical injury and accident. Since users become anesthetized, they may not realize that they are injured.
2. People who inhale the gas straight from the tank have been known to suffer frostbite of the nose, lips, and vocal cords, causing permanent damage.
3. Inhaling nitrous oxide (and all inhalants) can deprive the body of oxygen, resulting in unconsciousness or even death.
4. Prolonged use of nitrous oxide can interfere with the action of vitamin B_{12} in the body, resulting in damage to bone marrow and the nervous system and causing loss of sensation in the extremities, sometimes permanent.
5. Nitrous oxide can cause *cardiac arrhythmia* or *cardiac arrest.*
6. Chronic nitrous oxide abuse has been shown to cause *birth defects,* miscarriages, and *kidney* and *liver* damage.

Nonsteroidal Anti-inflammatory Drug

One of several *over-the-counter analgesics* that, in addition to relieving pain, reduce swelling from burns, sprains, broken bones, and other injuries. They are also used to treat chronic back pain, menstrual pain, headache, and pain resulting from minor surgery. Nonsteroidal anti-inflammatory drugs (NSAIDs) are particularly helpful in the treatment of arthritis (painful inflammation of the joints). *Aspirin* is the oldest and best known NSAID. The only over-the-counter analgesic that is not an NSAID is *acetaminophen*.

NSAIDs act by blocking the production of body chemicals called prostaglandins. These chemicals cause inflammation and send pain signals to the brain when someone is injured.

All NSAIDs, especially aspirin, can cause digestive problems, particularly peptic ulcers (open sores in the lining of the stomach). Some NSAIDs, such as *ibuprofen*, are less irritating to the stomach than aspirin. Taking NSAIDs with food may reduce the occurrence of digestive problems. NSAIDs may also cause indigestion, nausea, and diarrhea.

Novocaine

A local *anesthetic*. Novocaine is used to numb body parts before minor surgery and is most often used in dentistry. Alone, novocaine wears off in about fifteen minutes. Sometimes it is mixed with epinephrine; this combination produces analgesia (pain relief) for approximately forty-five minutes. Novocaine has been largely replaced by anesthetics that work faster and last longer, such as *lidocaine*.

Negative *side effects* of novocaine may include allergy symptoms, such as rash, itching, hives, and swelling of the mouth and throat. These symptoms can cause a blockage of the airways, becoming potentially life-threatening. Rare side effects may include drowsiness, ringing in the ears, and anxiety.

Novocaine was initially derived from *cocaine* in 1905. Prior to that time, cocaine was the anesthetic most doctors chose to use. Unlike cocaine, novocaine is not addictive.

Novocaine

See also:
Aspirin

See also:
Adrenaline

- Opiate/Opium
- Opioid Analgesic
- Overdose
- Over-the-Counter Drug
- Oxycodone

Opiate/Opium

Opium is a *drug* made from a milky substance produced by unripe poppy plants. The juice of the poppy plant is collected and dried to form a thick, brown, sticky liquid known as raw opium. Raw opium can be turned into a brownish powder called refined opium. Opium is actually a combination of many chemicals, including *morphine* and *codeine*. A strong *depressant,* it was popular as a pain reliever and *recreational drug* in the 1800s, especially in China, where it was commonly *smoked.* It can also be taken orally or *injected.*

Opiates (also called *narcotics*) are drugs derived from opium. Opiates act by affecting the same *receptors* that *endorphins* do. Morphine, a yellowish powder, is extracted from raw opium during the refining process. Many other opiates are derived from morphine, including codeine. Opiates can be naturally derived from opium and morphine, or they can be *synthetically* constructed in labs, like *fentanyl.*

Some opiates, known as *opioid analgesics,* are commonly prescribed to treat moderate to severe pain, persistent cough, and severe diarrhea, and are used as presurgery relaxants. Others, like *heroin* (one of the most powerful opiates), are illegal in the United States. These drugs and their derivatives are often abused for the *high* they produce. All opiates have the potential of being highly addictive.

A close-up of the poppy plant.

Opioid Analgesic

A *narcotic* prescribed to treat moderate to severe pain. These *drugs* may also be prescribed as *cough remedies* or as presurgery relaxants. Opioid analgesics can be taken orally or *injected.* The most common ones are *morphine* and *codeine.*

See also:
Opiate/Opium

Overdose

The *toxic* effects of taking too much of a *drug,* either accidentally or intentionally (in the case of suicide). Since most drugs are *poisons,* they can cause dangerous, often fatal, results in too large a *dose.*

Overdoses can happen for a number of reasons. People who frequently take particular drugs can build a *tolerance* for them. When they take larger doses to achieve results they once obtained with normal or prescribed doses, they may experience an overdose. Drug abusers sometimes take an excess of a drug, not knowing when to stop. Some people overdose purposely to commit suicide. Small children may overdose on *prescription drugs* when adults do not store the drugs properly.

The results of an overdose depend on the drug. Some common effects of overdose include *heart* rate fluctuations, *cardiac arrhythmia, heart failure,* breathing difficulty, permanent organ damage, *blackout, seizures, coma,* and death.

Over-the-Counter Drug

A *drug* that can be obtained without a doctor's *prescription.* The *FDA* decides which drugs are safe for over-the-counter sale and which should be classified as prescription drugs. Most drugs have the potential to cause ailments in at least some people. For example, while *aspirin* is considered a very safe over-the-counter drug, it can cause a rare, sometimes fatal disease known as Reye's syndrome in children who have influenza or chicken pox. The FDA, however, must decide if the risks of any given drug are small enough to let the population have access to it. The FDA also takes into consideration the drug's potential for abuse.

Typical over-the-counter drugs include *analgesics,* cold medicines, allergy medicines, *diet aids, motion sickness drugs, sleep aids,* and *antacids.*

It should be kept in mind that over-the-counter drugs can be dangerous if not taken according to the directions on the package. Some can cause an *overdose* if too much is taken; others can cause *addiction* if taken for an extended period of time. Always read the directions and precautions on the packages of over-the-counter drugs before taking them.

Oxycodone

A *synthetic opioid analgesic* whose effects are similar to those of *morphine*. Oxycodone is usually combined with an *analgesic*—especially *acetaminophen* (*Percocet*) and aspirin (*Percodan*)—to treat moderate to severe pain, as well as chronic pain. This *drug* is also helpful in relaxing people who are in pain. It is taken orally.

Like all *depressants,* oxycodone slows the *central nervous system.* Negative *side effects* include drowsiness, dry mouth, double vision, constipation, difficulty in urinating, dizziness, nausea, vomiting, *euphoria*, rash, itching, *cardiac arrhythmia,* and breathing difficulty. An *overdose* of oxycodone can cause drowsiness, cramps, nausea, vomiting, weakness, dizziness, bluish skin, *low blood pressure,* breathing difficulty, halted respiration, *liver* damage (often fatal), *seizures, blackout, coma,* and death. Long-term use of oxycodone can result in *lung* problems, *anemia,* and *heart* damage.

People who take medications that contain oxycodone for chronic pain can quickly become addicted. The drug can cause *physical* and *psychological dependence,* as well as *tolerance. Withdrawal* symptoms are similar to those of morphine.

P

- PCP
- Peer Pressure
- Penicillin
- Percocet
- Percodan
- Peyote
- Pharmaco-dynamics
- Pharmaco-kinetics
- Physical Dependence
- Pipe
- Placebo
- Pneumonia
- Poison/Poisoning
- Polysubstance Use
- "Poppers"
- Possession
- Pregnancy (effects of drugs on)
- Prescription Drug
- Prevention
- Prohibition
- Prozac
- Psilocybin
- Psychoactive Drug
- Psychological Dependence

PCP

Phencyclidine, or PCP, was developed in the 1950s as an *anesthetic* but was discontinued when physicians realized that it caused psychotic episodes in patients. PCP has since become one of the most dangerous street drugs. It can be taken orally, *smoked, snorted,* or *injected.* On the streets, PCP is often mixed with other drugs, such as *marijuana, cocaine,* and *crack.*

PCP

See also:
Adulterant

It is difficult to categorize PCP because it has characteristics of several kinds of drugs: *hallucinogens, depressants, stimulants, analgesics,* and anesthetics. In very low *doses,* it can have similar effects to marijuana, including lack of coordination and slurred speech. The larger the dose, however, the more dangerous and uncontrollable the *side effects.* Medium-sized doses can cause increased *heart* rate, increased blood pressure, lack of coordination, shallow breathing, sweating, nausea, vomiting, fatigue, blank stare, drooling, dizziness, confusion, and numbness. High doses can cause *low blood pressure,* muscle spasms, *heart failure, lung* failure, dangerously high fever, *stroke, seizures, blackout, coma,* and death. Large doses can cause psychotic behavior that lasts for two or three days, or longer. Regardless of the dose, PCP is known to cause bizarre and aggressive behavior in its users: violent mood swings, delusions, *hallucinations,* savage outbursts, inability to feel pain, schizophrenia, and jumbled speech. PCP use can lead to senseless, often fatal accidents (burns, car accidents, drownings) when users experience complete detachment from reality.

Long-term effects of PCP use include memory loss, speech defects, *depression,* malnutrition, loss of motor skills, mood swings, *flashbacks,* and schizophrenia. Prolonged use of PCP can also lead to *psychological dependence.* Users can build a *tolerance* for PCP, causing them to use increasingly larger doses. This can result in *overdose,* which is often fatal.

Peer Pressure

Feeling obligated to do what a peer group is doing in order to fit in. Peer pressure generally refers to teens who feel compelled to do things they would not do under normal circumstances. Most people, especially teens, have a desire to be a part of a group of people who share the same likes and dislikes and enjoy the same activities. When trying to fit into one of these groups, some people may feel pressure to try certain activities (often *drug, alcohol,* and *tobacco experimentation*), perhaps believing they will be rejected if they don't follow the group.

Penicillin

Peer pressure is of two types: negative peer pressure and positive peer pressure. Negative peer pressure, the kind already mentioned, is what most people think about when they hear the term "peer pressure." Many teens must deal with negative peer pressure at some point. They should remember that while everyone wants to be a part of a group, true friends would never expect them to do something they don't want to do.

Positive peer pressure refers to a situation in which friends urge a person to try something positive that he or she may not have thought of or had the courage to try before. For instance, someone who has never played a sport—and has never desired to do so—may enjoy playing softball only after being persuaded to join a summer team with friends.

Penicillin

Any of a group of *antibiotics* derived from certain molds and used to treat infections, including *pneumonia, bronchitis,* syphilis, and gonorrhea. Penicillin *drugs* were the first antibiotics ever developed. In 1928, a British scientist named Sir Alexander Fleming discovered penicillin accidentally. He found mold growing in a plate containing bacteria. The mold had destroyed the bacteria around it. Penicillin was field-tested during World War II and helped save the lives of many enlisted men.

Penicillin fights infections by destroying bacteria and preventing them from reproducing. Certain types of bacteria have developed resistance to penicillin. Scientists have countered this by developing *synthetic* penicillin drugs, but some strains of bacteria have grown resistant to these as well.

Alexander Fleming, the discoverer of penicillin, at work in his laboratory.

See also:
STD

Some people are allergic to penicillin, experiencing rash, vomiting, and diarrhea when taking it. An allergic reaction to penicillin may also cause constriction of the airways to the *lungs* and *low blood pressure,* which can result in dizziness, *blackout,* and death if not treated immediately.

Percocet

See *Oxycodone.*

Percodan

See *Oxycodone.*

Peyote

See *Mescaline.*

Pharmacodynamics

A term describing the way *drugs* affect the body. Some drugs are selective and affect only a specific organ. Others affect the body as a whole.

Most drugs cause changes in the body by attaching themselves (or binding) to certain *receptors* in the *central nervous system.* Drugs known as agonists stimulate receptors, mimicking the effects of a natural substance in the body. For instance, *opioids* bind to the same receptors as *endorphins,* and both have an *analgesic* (pain-relieving) effect on the body. Others, called antagonists, bind to receptors and block other natural substances from reaching those receptors. *Cocaine,* for example, binds to the receptors normally reserved for the neurotransmitter (chemical messenger) called *dopamine,* causing a buildup of dopamine in the central nervous system. This in turn causes the individual to feel an excess of the *euphoric* effects that dopamine usually has on the body. Drugs may also affect enzymes in the body in the same way. Enzymes carry drugs to different areas of the body. Some drugs do not directly affect receptors or enzymes, but initiate chemical reactions in certain areas of the body; *antacids* react with stomach acid and not with receptors.

Pharmacodynamics also includes the time it takes for drugs to affect the body, potency (the amount of the drug needed to have an effect), efficacy (the maximum effect the drug can have), affinity (how strongly the drug is attracted to the receptor), and the effects of different *doses.*

Pharmacokinetics

A term describing how the body deals with *drugs.* Administration describes how a drug enters the body: orally, by *injection,* sublingually (under the tongue), rectally, transdermally (through the skin), or by inhalation (through the *lungs*). Absorption refers to the rate and the extent to which a drug is taken in by the bloodstream. Distribution refers to the speed or slowness with which a drug makes its way through the body. Metabolism refers to the way drugs are chemically altered in the body. Elimination refers to the way the body rids itself of drugs.

See also:
Chemical Dependence
Delirium Tremens
Psychological Dependence

Physical Dependence

Habitual use of a *drug* can cause a person to become physically dependent on it, resulting in *tolerance* and in *withdrawal* symptoms when use is stopped. The body becomes accustomed to the presence of some drugs and eventually needs higher *doses* to achieve the same results. When the use is stopped abruptly, negative physical effects (withdrawal symptoms) occur; these effects depend on the particular drug but may include sweating, stomach cramps, insomnia, headache, nausea, vomiting, diarrhea, shaking, and fatigue.

Not all drugs lead to physical dependence. Some, like *marijuana*, are not believed to be physically addictive. Some, like *heroin* and *opium*-based drugs, have withdrawal symptoms that are severe but not life-threatening. Others, like *alcohol* and *barbiturates*, can cause life-threatening withdrawal symptoms, including tremors, *seizures, hallucinations,* and *coma.* Withdrawal symptoms that are difficult to withstand often lead to drug *relapse. Detoxification* is a common treatment for physical dependence.

Pipe

An instrument used to *smoke tobacco* and some *drugs.* Most pipes have a bowl in which the substance is placed to be burned, producing smoke to be inhaled. The bowl is connected to a length of hollow tubing, or stem, through which the smoke is drawn. The stem sometimes ends in a mouthpiece that is placed between the lips when inhaling.

A water pipe—also known as a hookah or bong—is constructed of a bowl, a stem, a container of water, and sometimes an additional stem or flexible tube. The smoke passes though the water to be cooled before it is inhaled.

Pipes are used to smoke a variety of drugs, particularly *marijuana* and *hashish,* and sometimes *cocaine* and *crack.*

Placebo

A substance, with no effect on the body, given to patients instead of an actual *drug.* Placebo pills are often made of sugar. Placebo *injections* may be saline water.

The effectiveness of a drug can be based on its "placebo effect," that is, the effects the patient believes will happen. Placebos are effective when the patient expects certain results. Changes come about as a result of a psychological state of mind and a trusting relationship between patient and doctor. Some researchers believe that merely expecting the "medication" to help causes the natural pain relievers in the body, called *endorphins,* to begin acting.

Pneumonia

See also:
Inhalant

Inflammation of the *lungs* from a viral or bacterial infection. Some cases of pneumonia can be caused by inhaling harmful chemicals or from *smoking.* Pneumonia can stem from some other affliction, for instance *alcoholism, AIDS, kidney* disease, *cancer,* or *diabetes.* Pneumonia is one of the leading causes of death in the United States.

Symptoms of pneumonia include fever, chills, breathing difficulty, and persistent coughing that produces a mucus called sputum. More serious symptoms include fluid in the lungs, chest pain, and pleurisy (inflammation of the membrane lining the lungs).

People with pneumonia may be able to rest at home but are often hospitalized for rest and treatment. *Drugs* are often administered, including *antibiotics* or *antifungal drugs,* and *NSAIDs* or *acetaminophen* to reduce fever. More severe cases may require oxygen therapy and artificial ventilation (use of a machine to aid respiration).

Poison/Poisoning

See also:
Overdose

A substance that causes illness when taken into the body. Poisons can be found in hundreds of household products, natural substances, industrial chemicals, and some foods. Some even originate in the body itself. *Drugs* and *alcohol* are considered poisons.

Poisons can be swallowed, absorbed through the skin, *injected,* and inhaled. Poisoning can be either acute (a large amount of poison entering the body in a short time) or chronic (small amounts of poison entering the body over a long period). Accidental poisoning is one of the most common types of poisoning. It can be the result of not reading labels on products, taking too large a *dose* of a drug, or children coming into contact with poisons they do not recognize. Prolonged exposure to harmful chemicals in the workplace is another common cause of poisoning.

Symptoms of poisoning depend on the substance and the individual. Some common effects include cramps, nausea, vomiting, headache, confusion, dizziness, fatigue, *cardiac arrhythmia,* breathing difficulty, *seizures, blackout, coma,* or death. Chronic poisoning can cause permanent organ damage.

Treatment for poisoning depends on the poison. Sometimes induced vomiting is recommended, but not for caustic substances or for people who are unconscious or having a seizure. CPR may be necessary. For poisons that come into contact with the skin or eyes, water should be flushed over the area immediately. Hospital treatment may include a process called gastric lavage, in which a tube is inserted into the stomach and the contents are removed. Other methods include *antidotes* and intravenous fluids to keep the patient hydrated and urinating to help eliminate the poison from the body.

Polysubstance Use

See also:
Drug Interaction

Use of more than one *drug* at one time. Taking two or more drugs can have a number of results. The drugs can cancel each other out and have no effects, although this type of reaction is rare. With drugs that produce similar effects (like *alcohol* and *barbiturates*), the reaction can be intensified, resulting in dangerous complications. Polysubstance use may also have unpredictable effects on the user, causing dangerous complications or no effects at all.

People who use illegal drugs may begin using two or more drugs when a *tolerance* is built for the initial drug. This is generally because the *high* from the initial drug is no longer satisfying, and a new way to achieve that high is sought. For example, people addicted to *heroin* often begin using other drugs, such as *cocaine,* when they build a tolerance for heroin. Others *experiment* with drug combinations to see what happens or to achieve highly *euphoric* or *intoxicating* sensations.

Some people find it necessary to take two or more *prescription* or *over-the-counter drugs*. A physician should be consulted before taking any drug and especially when mixing two or more drugs.

"Poppers"

See *Amyl Nitrite.*

Possession

A legal term that refers to the ownership of illegal *drugs*. People found with illegal drugs on their person (or in their cars or houses) are considered guilty of possession. The consequences of a possession charge depend on the drug, the quantity of the drug, and the state in which the individual is arrested. For instance, possession of *marijuana* is usually—but not always—considered a lesser crime than possession of a *hard drug* such as *heroin* or *LSD*. Punishment for possession may include a verbal warning, probation, monetary fine, repossession of property (automobile, for example), and jail time. In many states, merely being in the company of someone who is in possession of illegal drugs (even if you are unaware of that situation) makes you guilty of possession as well.

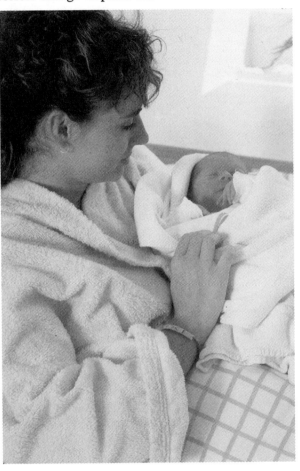

Pregnancy (effects of drugs on)

While some *drugs* are considered safe to use during pregnancy, pregnant women who use drugs run the risk of harming their unborn baby. Drug use can impair the mother's health, which can affect the development of the baby. Most substances that enter the mother's bloodstream will also enter the baby's bloodstream and can directly affect the baby's health.

Drugs and *alcohol* affect several stages of pregnancy. They impair the formation of organs at an early stage of fetal development. This can result in malformed organs and features, as well as miscarriage. As pregnancy continues, babies gain weight and their organs continue to develop. Drug use at this stage can cause low birth weight, early birth, and miscarriage. Drug use at the end of a pregnancy can result in low birth weight, difficult or painful delivery (for both mother and child), and other health problems for the baby (including *withdrawal* symptoms).

Alcohol consumption during pregnancy is the most common cause of mental retardation in babies; it can also lead to miscarriage, stillbirth, premature birth, physical defects, and withdrawal symptoms.

Drug use among pregnant women can cause serious problems in their children.

See also:
Birth Defects
Breast-Feeding
Fetal Alcohol Syndrome

See also:
Codeine

Pregnant women who *smoke cigarettes* commonly have babies with low birth weight. Even *secondhand smoke* can cause birth defects of the *heart,* brain, *lungs,* and face. These defects may be the result of carbon monoxide in the bloodstream; *nicotine* may prevent the fetus from receiving enough blood by constricting the blood vessels in the placenta.

Most (if not all) illegal drugs negatively affect the development of the fetus. Many *prescription* and *over-the-counter drugs* do the same. Avoidance of all drugs is best. Women should consult a doctor as soon as they know they are pregnant and should stop taking any unnecessary drugs.

Prescription Drug

A *drug* that cannot be legally obtained without the permission of a medical professional. Certain drugs may require a prescription because they are habit-forming, unpredictable, powerful, commonly abused, or used to treat an illness that must be supervised by a doctor.

After consultation, a doctor may fill out a prescription for a patient, which allows a pharmacist to give the patient the drugs indicated. Prescriptions also tell patients how large a *dose* they should take, how often, and for how long. Some drugs that normally require a prescription can be found in *over-the-counter drugs* (or nonprescription drugs) but in very small doses.

Some examples of prescription drugs include *antibiotics, barbiturates, benzodiazepines, hypnotic-sedatives, opioid analgesics,* and *tranquilizers.*

Prevention

A general term describing programs designed to help bring an end to illicit *drug* use. Most drug prevention programs focus on young children and teens, and work in conjunction with schools. These programs stress the harmful effects of drugs, the legal consequences of using illicit drugs, and the benefits of leading a life free from drugs, while involving students in hands-on activities and antidrug use community projects. Some school-based programs focus on children and teens who have already *experimented* with drugs, combining educational techniques with "scare tactics" (visiting prisons, probation, etc.). One of the most popular school drug-prevention programs, DARE (Drug Abuse Resistance Education), uses local law enforcement officials to help educate young students on the dangers of drug use.

Other drug prevention programs include health care programs designed to help people defeat drug habits and to remain *abstinent*. These programs may include government-funded *drug rehabilitation* centers, educational seminars, drug screening centers, Medicaid benefits, and clinics that supply aid to those who need health care (for example, *methadone* clinics). Law enforcement and punishment for drug users, *dealers,* and *drug traffickers* are also considered valuable tools in drug prevention, for both teens and adults. Youth offender programs are designed to incarcerate young drug users, but also to identify teens with the potential to become drug users and to educate them to the dangers of drug use. Last, drug use in the workplace is largely controlled with frequent *drug testing* and severe penalties (demotions and firing) for those who use drugs.

Prohibition

A law forbidding the production, transportation, or sale of *alcohol*. The most famous prohibition legislation is the Eighteenth Amendment to the Constitution, the Prohibition of Alcohol, which was ratified on January 29, 1919 and went into effect on January 29, 1920. In the years leading up to the enactment of the Eighteenth Amendment, medical professionals had begun to caution the country about negative health effects of drinking alcohol. Drinking alcohol also began to gain a reputation as a morally corrupt pastime. The U.S. government soon decided to enforce *abstinence* from alcohol across the nation. The Volstead Act or National Prohibition Act (passed by Congress in 1919) provided enforcement guidelines for the Eighteenth Amendment.

A man smashing a keg of beer during Prohibition.

The Eighteenth Amendment, however, failed to stamp out the consumption of alcohol in the United States. Over the next thirteen years, many Americans (known as bootleggers) continued to produce and transport alcohol to establishments that came to be called speakeasies. Speakeasies were notorious for wild parties involving alcohol, music, and dancing.

Because of a change in public opinion, as well as the inability of the government to curtail alcohol production and consumption, Congress passed the Twenty-first Amendment, the Repeal of Prohibition, in 1933. The Eighteenth Amendment is the only amendment ever to be repealed. Since then, *temperance* movements in the United States have pressured the government to reenact a similar form of prohibition, but without success. Some states, however, have placed more stringent restrictions on the production and sale of alcohol than others.

Prozac

The brand name of the *antidepressant* fluoxetine (specifically a *selective serotonin reuptake inhibitor*). Prozac is used to treat *depression,* obsessive-compulsive disorder, and bulimia (excessive eating, followed by self-induced vomiting). Prozac is taken orally and usually takes one to four weeks to become effective. It is not recommended to take Prozac for longer than six months.

Prozac works by raising the levels of *serotonin* in the *central nervous system.* Researchers believe that a lack of serotonin can lead to depression and other psychological disorders. Prozac is considered safer and more effective than other antidepressants because it causes fewer *side effects,* a special diet is not necessary (as with *monoamine oxidase inhibitors*), and an *overdose* is usually not fatal.

Prozac can also result in negative side effects, however, particularly nausea and vomiting (which should disappear after the first few days), headache, diarrhea, anxiety, nervousness, insomnia, sleepiness, and rash (sign of an allergic reaction). Sexual dysfunction is the most commonly reported side effect. Other side effects may include sweating, dry mouth, loss of appetite, weight loss, constipation, cramps, *seizures,* and *mania.* Some people have reported experiencing violent behavior and suicidal tendencies while taking Prozac; however, some researchers believe these reactions may be a result of depression and not Prozac. Others have reported *alcohol cravings* while taking Prozac.

The long-term effects of Prozac are not yet fully understood. Prozac has been found to encourage tumor growth in *cancer* patients, although it is not believed to cause cancer. Prozac may cause *tolerance* after approximately

Prozac comes in pill form and is taken orally.

six months, at which point the individual could *relapse* into depression. Prozac is not believed to cause *chemical dependence,* nor does it cause *withdrawal* symptoms when use is stopped abruptly.

Psilocybin

A *hallucinogen* found in certain mushrooms. Psilocybin and a closely related chemical called psilocin disrupt levels of *serotonin* and other neurotransmitters (chemical messengers) in the *central nervous system,* although researchers are not sure exactly how. Mushrooms containing psilocybin are usually dried and eaten, either alone or mixed with food. They are sometimes crushed to form a powder that can be *snorted.* Psilocybin has been *synthetically* manufactured in labs since the 1950s.

Like all hallucinogens, psilocybin is taken by many to induce *hallucinations* and *euphoria.* Users report unique feelings of awareness, relaxation, new perception, extreme sensations of compassion for others, and out-of-body experiences. Lights and colors may seem brighter, and objects may seem to move or "breathe." This *drug* may also cause nausea, vomiting, nervousness, visual disruptions (even when eyes are closed, called the "kaleidoscope effect"), poor perception of time, mood swings, *depression,* anxiety, slight rise in blood pressure and body temperature, feelings of power, and a general loss of control. Larger *doses* may cause more disruptive *side effects.* First-time users who are not prepared for the effects of psilocybin may experience a "bad *trip,*" negative mental effects, including attacks of paranoia and feelings of anxiety or fear (although this can happen to anyone using the drug, even experienced users). *Overdose* on this drug is highly unlikely.

Although psilocybin is comparable to *LSD* and *peyote,* it is believed to be safer than most hallucinogens. Accidents, as a result of impaired judgment and altered perceptions, are perhaps the most common negative effect. There are no known long-term effects, but people who take psilocybin for an extended period of time may experience *flashbacks* weeks, months, or even years after they stop using it. Psilocybin is not believed to cause *chemical dependence.*

Psychoactive Drug

A *drug* (prescribed or *recreational*) that affects an individual psychologically. Psychoactive drugs may cause changes in mood, behavior, thinking, or perception. They act by affecting the levels of neurotransmitters (chemical messengers) found in the *central nervous system.* The following drug

categories contain psychoactive drugs: *alcohol, stimulants, depressants, hypnotic-sedatives* (including *barbiturates, benzodiazepines,* and *tranquilizers*), *antidepressants, opioid analgesics,* and *hallucinogens.*

Psychological Dependence

The urge to continue using a particular *drug* because of an effect it has on the user. These desired effects may include reduced anxiety and/or tension, *euphoria* and/or *intoxication,* and improved physical and/or mental performance (perceived or actual). Psychological dependence can dominate a person's life, resulting in *depression, compulsive behavior,* absence from work/school, problems with family and friends, and other social and personal difficulties. Psychological dependence can hinder many areas of a person's life, especially when obtaining and using the drug in question is all the individual can think about.

Unlike *physical dependence,* almost all drugs—especially *recreational drugs*—have the ability to cause psychological dependence. Most *drug rehabilitation* programs are designed to help manage the results of psychological dependence. These rehabilitation methods may include counseling, medical treatment, and *twelve-step programs.*

See also:
Chemical Dependence

Q

- Quaalude
- Quinine

Quaalude

The brand name of the *hypnotic-sedative* methaqualone. Quaaludes were once commonly prescribed as *tranquilizers* to reduce tension but have been replaced by safer, less addictive *drugs*. Methaqualone and *glutethimide* were developed in the 1960s as *barbiturate* alternatives but were found to be more dangerous and addictive. Quaaludes can be taken orally or *injected*, and the effects last four to eight hours.

Like all *depressants*, Quaaludes slow down the *central nervous system*, resulting in relaxation in lower *doses*, and *intoxication* in higher doses. Other *side effects* include *euphoria*, lack of inhibitions, slurred speech, dizziness, nausea, vomiting, mood swings, *depression*, lack of coordination, decreased heartbeat, and decreased breathing. An *overdose* of Quaaludes can result in cold and clammy skin, shallow breathing, *cardiac arrhythmia*, *blackouts*, *coma*, and death.

Prolonged Quaalude use can result in *physical* and *psychological dependence*, as well as *tolerance.Withdrawal* symptoms may include anxiety, insomnia, delirium, *seizures*, and possibly death. Much like the withdrawal symptoms of barbiturates, Quaalude withdrawal is said to be more severe than *heroin* withdrawal.

Through the 1960s and 70s, Quaaludes were abused by young people seeking an intense *high*. They were sometimes mixed with *alcohol* to achieve heightened intoxication, which made them even more dangerous and resulted in many overdoses. Some people have even smoked a mixture of *marijuana* and Quaaludes. Quaaludes have been illegal in the United States since 1984 and are considered to have no medicinal value.

Quinine

A *drug* derived from the bark of the cinchona tree used primarily to treat malaria (a disease transmitted by mosquitoes, especially in tropical locations, that can result in death). This drug reduces fever due to malaria and helps kill certain parasites in the blood. Low *doses* of quinine are sometimes used to treat nighttime leg cramps. A derivative of quinine (quinidine) is sometimes used to treat *cardiac arrhythmia*. Quinine can also be found in a product called tonic water, which is commonly mixed with *alcohol* to give it a bitter taste. A number of *synthetic* versions of quinine have been developed since World War II, when there was a shortage of this drug. They are usually more expensive and less effective (because of resistant strains of malaria), but are less dangerous than quinine.

Negative *side effects* of quinine may include cramps, sleepiness, difficulty sleeping, hunger, nausea, vomiting, diarrhea, anxiety, blurred vision, cold and clammy skin, fever and chills, headache, difficulty in concentrating, *hypoglycemia*, mood swings, blood in the urine and stool, confusion, and increased *heart* rate. Rare side effects may include breathing difficulty, changes in color vision, double vision, hives, rash, swelling around the eyes and mouth, muscle cramps, and ringing in the ears. A quinine *overdose* may result in blindness, double vision, hearing problems, dizziness, *blackout*, increased heart rate, heart problems, cardiac arrhythmia, *seizures*, and *coma*.

Scraping the bark of the cinchona tree in order to derive quinine.

147

R

- Receptor
- Recovery
- Recreational Drug Use
- Relapse
- Ritalin
- Rohypnol

Receptor

Nerve cells in the sensory organs (skin, eyes, ears, tongue, nasal membrane) that convert external stimuli into electrical impulses; or a particular area on the surface of neurons (nerve cells) that helps convey information from neuron to neuron with the aid of neurotransmitters (chemical messengers) and other chemicals.

Receptors can be thought of as openings on each neuron into which neurotransmitters and hormones fit. Most receptors accept only one type of neurotransmitter. Neurotransmitters and receptors fit together like keys in locks. These keys and locks form a system that conveys messages throughout the nervous system. When this process is triggered in the brain by external stimuli, an individual experiences an emotional response or a physical reaction.

Many *drugs* bind, or attach, themselves to certain receptors, influencing the way neurotransmitters work. *Cocaine,* for example, binds to *dopamine* receptors. This results in a buildup of dopamine in the synapses, or spaces, between neurons, causing a cocaine *high.*

Although receptors have natural purposes, some drugs take advantage of them, causing similar reactions within the body. For example, *narcotics* bind to the same receptors to which *endorphins* bind. Both substances result in a reduction of pain and even a state of *euphoria.* In the case of the narcotic *morphine,* doctors have used this situation to advantage, since morphine is a valuable tool in treating moderate to severe pain. The narcotic *heroin,* on the other hand, is commonly abused for its euphoric effects and has no medical value.

Receptor

See also:
Central Nervous System

Recovery

A term referring to the process of ending a *drug addiction* and attaining a state of *sobriety.* Recovery usually entails a number of *drug rehabilitation* programs and methods.

See also:
Stages of Drug Use

Recreational Drug Use

Sometimes called social drug use or social drinking, this term refers to the use of *drugs* and *alcohol* in a social setting. Recreational drug use usually pertains to people who drink alcohol or use *soft drugs* with friends, often at parties, small gatherings, or a bar. Recreational drug users usually do not exhibit the problems that afflict habitual or addicted drug users (absence from work, falling grades, lack of responsibility, frequent use of drugs while alone, withdrawal from society, mood swings, *depression,* etc.).

This type of drug use usually begins with *experimentation* (perhaps as a result of negative *peer pressure*), but it can develop into a more dangerous problem. Most recreational drugs are also considered *gateway drugs,* particularly alcohol, *tobacco,* and *marijuana.*

Relapse

Drug addictions can be very difficult to overcome, despite modern *drug rehabilitation* methods and programs. When a person who is going through or has finished drug rehabilitation begins using drugs again, he or she is said to have a relapse.

Relapse may occur when addicts cannot withstand the physical and psychological effects of *withdrawal.* Depending on the drug, withdrawal symptoms can range from mild to life-threatening. Withdrawal from *narcotics,* for example, is usually not life-threatening but can be quite severe and may include flulike symptoms such as nausea, vomiting, fatigue, headaches, and *depression.* These symptoms can last two weeks or longer and are often the reason for relapse.

Some people, however, may relapse months, even years after the withdrawal symptoms have disappeared, despite knowing the dangers associated with drug use. The reasons for this development may include social pressures, family hardships, and depression. Others may simply enjoy the *euphoric* or *intoxicating* effects so much that they cannot refrain from using drugs, even after experiencing rehabilitation and dangerous complications. For these people, *twelve-step programs* may help overcome the urge to begin using drugs again. Twelve-step programs such as *Alcoholics Anonymous* provide drug users with an ongoing forum to discuss the difficulties of remaining *sober.*

Ritalin

The brand name of the *prescription drug* methylphenidate. Ritalin is a *central nervous system stimulant* that reduces hyperactivity and increases concentration in people who have attention deficit disorder (ADD) or attention deficit hyperactivity disorder (ADHD). Its stimulant properties make it appropriate for treating narcolepsy (sudden daytime sleep). This *drug* is most often taken orally; it can be *injected* into the body, but this method has been found to block blood vessels in the eyes and *lungs.*

Negative *side effects* of Ritalin include nausea, vomiting, loss of appetite, weight loss, insomnia, nervousness, stomach cramps, headaches, drowsiness, dizziness, mood swings, rash, fever, *cardiac arrhythmia,* and changes in blood pressure. Some patients report the development of tics and uncontrollable movements (clinically known as Tourette's syndrome). In rare circumstances, patients have developed *liver* damage, *anemia,* and hair loss. An *overdose* of Ritalin can result in nausea, vomiting, irritability, muscle spasms, *euphoria,* confusion, stuttering, *hallucinations,* delirium, cardiac arrhythmia, *seizures,* and *coma.*

Ritalin can potentially lead to *physical* and *psychological dependence,* as well as *tolerance* (*addiction* rates are lower for children than they are for adults). *Withdrawal* symptoms of Ritalin usually include *depression,* trouble in concentrating, and fatigue.

It has recently been discovered that Ritalin affects the brain similarly to *cocaine* and *amphetamines* and may lead to future addictions. Like these illegal drugs, Ritalin is sometimes abused for its euphoric effects, even though it is difficult to obtain without a prescription. Ritalin has become a commonly abused drug among children and teens; those who have ADD and ADHD are pressured to give their medication to others who will abuse it. People abuse Ritalin to improve their physical or mental performance or to stay awake longer. A Ritalin *high,* however, often results in a *crash,* and users may experience depression and other psychological difficulties when the drug wears off. In rare cases Ritalin abuse has been linked to death.

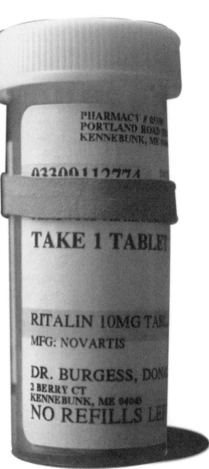

Ritalin is primarily prescribed for children and teens.

Rohypnol

The brand name of the *benzodiazepine* flunitrazepam, which is marketed in Latin America and Europe as a *sleep aid* but is illegal in the United States. Rohypnol is similar to the *tranquilizer Valium* but about ten times more powerful. This *drug* is taken orally, takes about thirty minutes to affect the user, and can last up to eighty hours depending on the *dose*.

Like all *hypnotic-sedatives*, Rohypnol produces relaxation in small doses and sedation in larger doses. Other *side effects* include *intoxication, euphoria,* loss of inhibitions, poor motor skills, dizziness, sleepiness, irritability, aggressive behavior, headache, nausea, vomiting, decreased blood pressure, *blackout*, amnesia, *hallucinations,* delusions, tremors, and confusion. A Rohypnol *overdose* may include drowsiness, confusion, sluggishness, respiratory depression, *coma,* and, rarely, death, especially when combined with other *depressants*.

Frequent use of Rohypnol can result in *physical* and *psychological* *dependence*. *Withdrawal* symptoms may include headache, muscle cramps, anxiety, numbness, tingling in the hands and feet, confusion, hallucinations, and *seizures*. Treatment for Rohypnol *addiction* may include *detoxification* with a drug called phenobarbital, another benzodiazepine.

Rohypnol is sometimes mixed with other drugs (such as *heroin* and *alcohol*) to enhance the *high* of both drugs. Although Rohypnol rarely results in death from overdose, it can be deadly when mixed with other drugs. This drug is also known as a *date-rape drug,* slipped into drinks with the intent of sedating a person before sexual assault. In some countries, Rohypnol is used to treat the withdrawal symptoms of other drugs, putting the user into an apathetic state.

S

- Seconal
- Secondhand Smoke
- Seizure
- Selective Serotonin Reuptake Inhibitor (SSRI)
- Serotonin
- Side Effect
- Signs of Drug Use
- Sinsemilla
- Slang Terms
- Sleep Aid
- Smoke/Smoking
- Snort
- Sober/Sobriety
- Soft Drug
- Stages of Drug Use
- STD
- Steroid
- Stimulant
- Stroke
- Sudden Sniffing Death (SSD)
- Synergism
- Synthetic Drug

Seconal

Seconal

The brand name of the *barbiturate* secobarbital, which is very similar to *Amytal*. Seconal is used to treat insomnia and to calm and sedate patients before surgery and dental operations. It can be taken orally or *injected*.

Secondhand Smoke

See also:
Nicotine

Sometimes referred to as environmental *tobacco smoke*, secondhand smoke is tobacco smoke that is involuntarily inhaled, especially by a nonsmoker. There are two types of secondhand smoke. Mainstream smoke is the smoke exhaled by a smoker. Sidestream smoke is the smoke that comes from a burning tobacco product.

People who inhale secondhand smoke (called passive smokers) are subject to the same dangers as regular smokers. Although secondhand smoke is less concentrated than smoke directly inhaled from a tobacco product, passive smokers can develop respiratory problems, *lung cancer,* and cardiovascular problems after long exposure.

Secondhand smoke has been found particularly dangerous for very young children. Young children exposed to it can develop respiratory infections, reduced lung volume, constricted arteries, persistent coughs, more frequent colds, asthma, and ear infections, and be at higher risk for sudden infant death syndrome (SIDS).

Seizure

Abnormal electrical activity in the brain. Epilepsy is a condition character-ized by recurring seizures. Some people have seizures all their lives; others may have one and never experience another.

Depending on the severity of the seizure, a person may experience tin-gling, odd smells or tastes, convulsions (jerking muscles), *hallucinations,* confusion, and *blackout.* Strange sensations may be experienced before and after a seizure; strange lights and *euphoria,* for example. These effects can be pleasurable or frightening. After a seizure, people do not usually remember what happened when they regain consciousness, which generally occurs in about five minutes.

Seizures have many causes, including high fever, infection of the tissues surrounding the brain, lack of oxygen reaching the brain, *stroke*, brain tumor, head injury, *liver* failure, *kidney* failure, *hypoglycemia*, *hyperglycemia*, ingestion of *toxic* substances, adverse reactions to *drugs*, and *withdrawal* from drugs.

Drugs used to treat chronic seizures are called anticonvulsants. *Luminal* is an anticonvulsant.

Selective Serotonin Reuptake Inhibitor (SSRI)

A class of *antidepressants* used primarily to treat *depression*. SSRIs are also used to treat obsessive-compulsive disorder (being burdened by unwanted thoughts and/or the compulsion to repeat certain activities due to an irrational fear), panic disorder, social phobias, and bulimia.

SSRIs raise the levels of the neurotransmitters (chemical messengers) in the brain that the body uses to fight depression and other mental illnesses. It commonly takes two to three weeks for the positive effects of SSRIs to set in.

SSRIs are relatively safer than other antidepressants, having fewer and less harmful *side effects*. Short-term effects of SSRIs include nausea, diarrhea, headache, nervousness, loss of coordination, jitteriness, insomnia, tremors, and sexual dysfunction. Reports of *overdoses* are rare.

Tolerance and *addiction* to SSRIs are rare. Most problems occur when the person fails to take a large enough *dose* or abruptly stops using an SSRI. At this point, *withdrawal* symptoms may occur, including nausea, vomiting, cramps, diarrhea, chills, insomnia, and anxiety.

Serotonin

A substance in the body that has several functions, one of which is reducing blood loss due to injury. Serotonin also acts as a neurotransmitter (chemical messenger) in the *central nervous system*. Researchers believe that serotonin affects one's moods and perception of the world.

People with psychological problems such as obsessive-compulsive disorder and *depression* are believed to have insufficient levels of serotonin and other neurotransmitters. Doctors sometimes prescribe *drugs* that increase amounts of serotonin, alleviating negative psychological problems.

See also:
Antidepressant
Mania
Selective Serotonin
Reuptake Inhibitor

Some *recreational drugs* are believed to alter perceptions by affecting the way serotonin acts. *Hallucinogens* such as *LSD* and *MDMA* are known to cause *hallucinations,* mood swings, and altered perceptions by raising the levels of serotonin in the central nervous system.

Side Effect

A reaction to a *drug* in addition to the effect the drug is intended to produce. Also known as an adverse drug reaction, a side effect is most often considered a negative development.

There are two main types of side effects. The first is called the predictable side effect, which medical professionals expect when most people take a particular drug. An example of a predictable side effect is *low blood pressure* as a result of taking an *opioid analgesic.* Although this type of side effect is predictable, it is also usually unavoidable.

The second type is the unpredictable side effect, which occurs in a minority of people taking the drug and is caused by factors in the patient. It is considered unpredictable until a doctor can discover exactly what causes it. Common unpredictable side effects include *jaundice, kidney* disease, *anemia,* allergic reactions, rash, and swelling of the face and lips.

A particular drug reaction can be categorized either as an intended reaction or an adverse drug reaction, depending on the condition the drug is being used to treat. *Antihistamines,* for example, cause drowsiness. When used as a *sleep aid,* drowsiness is the intended reaction. When used to treat allergies, however, drowsiness is a side effect because it is not the effect the drug was intended to produce.

Side effects can be mild, moderate, or severe. Mild side effects, such as headache or upset stomach, are usually harmless. Severe side effects are considered life-threatening.

Signs of Drug Use

The following table is a list of potential signs of *intoxication.* (General signs of drug use may include sudden occurrences of anger and mood swings, paranoia, lack of responsibility, absence from work/school, poor physical condition, poor hygiene, wearing sunglasses often, borrowing money frequently, stealing, and lying.)

Signs of Drug Use

Drug	Physical	Other
Alcohol	Clumsiness, flushed face, loud speech, fatigue, red eyes, nausea, vomiting, slurred speech, deep sleep	Talkativeness, depression, mood swings, poor memory, aggressive behavior, breath and clothes smelling of alcohol, fake ID
Amphetamines	Dilated pupils, sweating, nausea, vomiting, confusion, weight loss, constant movement, grinding of teeth	Aggressive behavior, anger, anxiety, insomnia, loss of appetite, talkativeness
Cocaine/Crack	Dilated pupils, hyperactivity, jitteriness, sniffing or coughing, red nose, weight loss, high blood pressure, seizures	Insomnia, paranoia, loss of appetite, aggressive behavior, anger, depression, nervousness
Depressants	Clumsiness, slurred speech, sleepiness, dilated pupils	Lack of concentration, depression, mood swings
Hallucinogens	Glazed eyes, dilated pupils, hyperactivity, clumsiness, slurred speech	Irrational behavior/conversation, confusion, lack of concentration, paranoia, mood swings, self-absorption, unusual interest in ordinary objects
Heroin	Needle tracks on arms and legs, red nose, stupor, glazed-over eyes, staring, nausea, vomiting, cold and clammy skin, dilated pupils, sweating	Lack of response, frequent sleeping, loss of appetite, strange sleeping schedule
Inhalants	Unsteady movement, dizziness, nausea, vomiting, tremors, slurred speech, stupor, rolling eyes, watery eyes	Anger, apathy, unresponsiveness, paint on nose from inhaling, chemical smells, poor memory
Marijuana	Dry mouth, red eyes, narrow eyes, hunger, poor coordination, slow movements, clumsiness	Paranoia, anxiety, uncontrollable laughing, marijuana smell on clothes
Stimulants	Talkativeness, dilated pupils, weight loss, dry mouth, jittery movements	Irritability, paranoia, strange sleeping schedule, depression, aggressive behavior, anger, mood swings
Tobacco	Persistent cough, weight loss, frequent loss of breath, stained fingers and teeth, bad breath	Tobacco odor, frequent brushing of teeth and washing of hands

Sinsemilla

Female *marijuana* plants that have not been pollinated by male plants. Female marijuana plants have a higher concentration of *THC,* the active ingredient in marijuana. Marijuana cultivators have learned that by killing the male plants they can grow female plants without seeds. This causes development of larger buds, or flowers. The buds of the female plant have the highest concentration of THC and are therefore more valuable to growers and users. (Sinsemilla is Spanish for "without seeds.")

The sinsemilla plant.

Slang Terms

Most *drugs* have a slang, or street, name by which they are known to users and *dealers*. This table lists common illicit drugs and their slang names.

Substance	Slang Terminology
Alcohol	Booze, juice, sauce
Amphetamines	Amy, army, poppers
Amyl nitrite	Blue heavens, yellow jackets
Amytal	Mollies, black beauties, speed, uppers, bennies
Anabolic steroids	Andro
Barbiturates	Barbs, downers, goofballs
Butyl nitrite	Rush, locker room
Chloral hydrate	Jellies, jelly beans, knockout drops, a Mickey, torpedo
Cocaine	Coke, snow, blow, toot, nose candy
Codeine	Schoolboy, Cody, C
Crack	Rock, crumbs, pebbles, bones
Designer drugs	Adam and Eve, Ecstasy, XTC, X, Goodfella, Crystal, Polo
Dilaudid	Juice, dillies, lords, little D, big D
DMT	Businessman's trip, Disneyland
Ephedrine	Now, herbal fuel, blasting caps
Fentanyl	Apache, China White, Tango and Cash, murder, poison, TNT
GHB	Easy lay, liquid X, grievous bodily harm, Georgia home boy
Glutethimide	Glue
Heroin	Horse, smack, H, speedball (mixed with cocaine)
Joint	J, spliff, doobie, blunt, twist one (to roll a joint)
Ketamine	Special K, vitamin K, kit-kat, jet fuel, cat valium
Librium	Downs, nerve pills, tranks, goofers, liberty, gone time
LSD	Acid, blotter, electric Kool-Aid, tabs, trips
Luminal	Downers, goofballs
Marijuana	Grass, pot, weed, ganja, Mary Jane, smoke
MDMA	Ecstasy, Adam, love drug
Mescaline	Buttons, big chief, cactus
Methadone	Dollies, meth, juice, done, dolls, fizzies
Methamphetamine	Uppers, snot, glue, ice, crystal, meth, speed, crank, glass
Morphine	M, morph, mother, sister, mud, dreamer
Nembutal	Nembies, yellow jackets
Nitrous oxide	Balloons, whip-its, laughing gas
Opium	Big O, dopium, tar, blackjack
PCP	Angel dust, hog, squeeze, whack, space base (mixed with crack)
Psilocybin	Magic mushrooms, shrooms, mushies, silly putty
Quaalude	Ludes, quay, quads, disco biscuits
Ritalin	Vitamin R, skippy, smart drug
Rohypnol	Roofies, roach, rope, rib, Mexican Valium
Seconal	Reds, red birds, red devils, barbs, Mexican reds, red bullets
Thorazine	Head on a post, zombie juice
Tuinal	Christmas tree, rainbows, double trouble, reds and blues, twoies
Xanax	Downs, nerve pills, tranks

Sleep Aid

A *drug* used to treat insomnia or anxiety disorders that prevent sleep. Mild sleep aids can be purchased in pharmacies. *Over-the-counter* sleep aids contain *antihistamines*, which are primarily used to treat allergy symptoms. Antihistamines naturally cause sleepiness. Some people (particularly the elderly) may experience negative *side effects*, such as constipation, blurred vision, ringing in the ears, and accidents resulting from a lack of coordination.

Prescription sleep aids include *hypnotic-sedatives, barbiturates, benzodiazepines, tranquilizers, antidepressants,* and *chloral hydrate.* Of these, benzodiazepines are most commonly prescribed for insomnia and are considered the least dangerous.

Sleep aids can cause *physical* and *psychological dependence. Tolerance* to sleep aids can result in a dangerous increase in *dosage,* sometimes resulting in *overdose. Withdrawal* from sleep aids can result in insomnia and anxiety. Sleep aids should not be taken for longer than two to three weeks and should not be taken every night. Sleep aids should not be mixed with other drugs, especially other *depressants* such as *alcohol.*

Smoke/Smoking

See also:
Ice
Joint
Pipe

The dense, *toxic* vapors caused by burning a *drug,* or the act of inhaling those vapors. Smoke is made up of solid and gas particles. When inhaled, the solid particles can be very harmful to the *lungs.*

Smoking most frequently refers to *cigarettes* and *tobacco.* Cigarette smoking is the most common cause of lung *cancer.* Drugs that are commonly smoked to induce *intoxication* and/or *euphoria* include *marijuana, freebase cocaine, crack,* and *peyote.* Other drugs that can be smoked include *methamphetamine, PCP, psilocybin, opium,* and other *narcotics.* Smoking any drug can lead to lung damage, respiratory problems, and cardiovascular problems, among other negative *side effects.*

Snort

To inhale sharply through the nose. Certain *drugs* (especially *cocaine*) are snorted and absorbed into the bloodstream through the nasal linings. Some users crush drugs that come in pill form so that they can be snorted. Snorted drugs affect the user more quickly than those that are swallowed. Other drugs that are sometimes snorted include *caffeine, ephedrine,* and *methamphetamine.* Snorting drugs can lead to nosebleeds, headache, sore throat, and permanently damaged nasal membranes.

Sober/Sobriety

Someone who is sober is not under the influence of any *intoxicating* or *euphoric drugs.* This term is most often used to describe a person who is not intoxicated on *alcohol,* but it is also used to describe *abstinence* from any intoxicating drug.

Sobriety refers to the state of being sober. People who are members of *Alcoholics Anonymous* strive for sobriety as a way of life after having abused alcohol for a period of time.

Soft Drug

A general term applied to *drugs* that are believed to be less harmful than others. *Marijuana, alcohol,* and *tobacco* are sometimes referred to as soft drugs. They supposedly lead to physical and mental damage less often than *hard drugs.* They might also lead to *overdose* less often.

The boundary between soft drugs and hard drugs is hazy at best. Some so-called soft drugs can lead to the same results as hard drugs (*physical* and *psychological dependence, tolerance,* overdose, or death). Tobacco, for instance, might be considered a soft drug by many, but *cigarettes* are the single largest cause of *lung cancer* in the United States. By categorizing drugs as either soft or hard, many *drug abuse* experts believe we are designating which drugs are okay for young people to *experiment* with, and which should be avoided altogether. The truth is that all drugs can be harmful if taken in large enough quantities or for an extended period of time.

Stages of Drug Use

The following table outlines the stages of *drug* use. While these general stages pertain to most drug users (teens and adults), this table focuses on teen drug use.

Stage	Description
Experimentation	Recreational drug use. Usually begins with peers, perhaps as a result of peer pressure. Often a sign of rebelliousness against authority figures. May not occur on a daily basis; often on weekends and vacations. Usually does not interfere with work/school.
Habitual Use	Drug use nearly every day. Uses drugs to feel good. May worry about losing drug source. May change friends to facilitate drug habit. Further separation from family and increased rebelliousness. Absence from work/school. Falling grades. Pride in increased drug tolerance.
Fixation	Loss of motivation, resulting in poor grades and attendance. Obvious behavioral changes. Drug use becomes a number-one priority. Strange or secretive actions, including lying. Dealing may begin to facilitate drug habit. Hard drug use and legal complications may occur.
Chemical Dependency	Inability to make it through everyday activities without drugs. Frequent paranoia. Denial of problem. Poor physical condition. Poor grades, dropping out of school. Constant intoxication. Depression, reckless behavior, and suicidal tendencies. Financial and legal problems. Loss of contact with friends and family.

See also:
AIDS
HIV

STD

A sexually transmitted disease is a disease spread during unprotected sex. Some STDs are life-threatening. STDs can be spread during illicit *drug* use, especially when sharing needles to *inject* drugs. Drug use has been found to increase sexual activity in general, as well as carelessness with regard to safe sex. These factors often result in the transmission of STDs. The following table describes the most common STDs.

STD	Symptoms	Treatment	Curable?
Chlamydia	Painful urination, swollen testicles, vaginal bleeding, itching genitals, fever, nausea, cramps	Prescription antibiotics; failure to treat early may result in sterility	Easily, but difficult to diagnose
Crabs (pubic lice)	Lice infestation of pubic hair, itching (a reaction to lice bites), reddened skin, inflammation	Over-the-counter topical creams and shampoos, cleaning clothes and bed sheets	Easily
Gonorrhea ("the clap")	Cloudy discharge from the penis or vagina, cramps, painful urination, inflamed genitals	Prescription antibiotics; failure to treat early may result in sterility	Yes, but some strains are resistant to drugs
Hepatitis B	Fever, hives, fatigue, nausea, vomiting, loss of appetite, jaundice, liver damage	Prescription drugs, altered diet, cleanliness	No, but can be prevented with vaccine
Herpes	Red and sensitive skin around genitals or mouth, bumpy skin, blisters, painful sores, flulike symptoms	Prescribed drugs, cleanliness, abstinence from sex during outbreaks to avoid spreading the disease	No; lies dormant in the body and may recur several times a year
Human Papillomavirus (HPV)	Genital warts and other growths, itching, soreness; can lead to cancer if not treated properly	Antiviral drugs, application of chemicals (usually acid) to remove	Yes, but recurrence is common
Syphilis	Sores on genitals, discolored patches on hands and feet, hair loss, rash, liver damage, brain damage, heart disease, paralysis	Penicillin, cleanliness; when not treated early, this disease can be fatal	Yes, but early treatment is vital

Steroid

A type of medication similar to the hormones secreted by the adrenal glands. The adrenal glands are located above the *kidneys* and reproductive organs and secrete dozens of these hormones to regulate several functions of the body, including the *immune system*, metabolism, salt and water balance, and the development of sexual traits. Some hormones also allow the body to withstand pain from injury or illness.

See also:
Anabolic Steroid

There are three types of medical steroids. Corticosteroids act like the hormones cortisone and hydrocortisone to control inflammation and pain. Corticosteroids are used medically, usually by *injection,* and are the most commonly prescribed steroids for medical conditions. People who take corticosteroids regularly have been known to exhibit one (rarely more) of the following symptoms: accumulations of fat in the abdomen, face, and neck; *hyperglycemia*; *diabetes*; muscular weakness; osteoporosis; joint damage; cataracts; easy bruising; slow-healing wounds; *hypertension;* weakened immune system; and mood swings.

Estrogenic steroids are similar to the hormones estrogen and progesterone, which are produced primarily by the ovaries. Birth control pills are estrogenic steroids. Estrogenic steroids are prescribed for women whose ovaries have been removed for medical reasons. This type of steroid has no potential for *substance abuse.*

The last type, *anabolic steroids,* are very similar to the hormone testosterone, which is produced in the male testes. Anabolic steroids help build muscle and tendon strength and are used medically to treat patients with *cancer* and *AIDS.* Anabolic steroids have a high potential for substance abuse.

Stimulant

Any *drug* that speeds up the *central nervous system.* Stimulants include *caffeine, nicotine,* some *diet aids, cocaine, amphetamines, MDMA,* and *PCP.* Stimulants act by increasing certain neurotransmitters (chemical messengers) in the central nervous system.

Stimulants prescribed to treat obesity speed up the central nervous system, provide extra energy, and suppress appetite. Other stimulants are used to improve breathing in people experiencing respiratory problems. Narcolepsy (sudden daytime sleep) is also treated with stimulants. Some stimulants are used to treat hyperactivity in children, although researchers do not know exactly why or how they seem to have a calming effect on these children.

Most stimulants increase concentration and physical performance and reduce sleepiness (and are often abused for these reasons). Stimulants can also cause nervousness, sweating, irritability, *cardiac arrhythmia, hypertension,* insomnia, fever, *hallucinations,* malnutrition, aggressive behavior, *blackout,* and *seizures.* Long-term *side effects* may include nerve damage, *kidney* damage, *liver* damage, *lung* problems, *heart attacks, heart failure,* chronic *depression,* and death.

Stimulants often cause extreme mood swings. Stimulant *highs*—especially those associated with cocaine and amphetamines—can be intensely *euphoric*. When the high wears off, however, the user usually experiences an equally intense *crash* involving depression and fatigue. Many users try to avoid the crash by taking larger *doses* of the drug more often. This can lead to *physical* and *psychological dependence, tolerance,* and *overdose*. *Withdrawal* symptoms may include sleepiness, headache, hunger, anxiety, and depression.

Most stimulants are considered *recreational drugs* or drugs of abuse. Cocaine (once a popular *anesthetic*) is a widely abused drug in the United States. Some people use cocaine many times a day, even when they are at work. Amphetamines (especially *methamphetamine* and MDMA) are abused by people who go to raves (all-night dances) and parties because of the extra energy they provide and their euphoric effects. Caffeine, the most popular stimulant in the world, is present in coffee, tea, soda, and chocolate.

Stroke

Damaged brain tissue resulting from interrupted oxygen supply to the brain (usually as a result of a blood clot) or a ruptured blood vessel that causes bleeding in the brain. Stroke may be caused by *hypertension, heart* disease, *diabetes mellitus,* atherosclerosis (blocked arteries), high cholesterol, *smoking,* and old age.

The symptoms of stroke take from a few minutes to a few days to develop, but they usually develop quickly. Strokes range from mild (sometimes barely noticeable) to severe. A stroke can result in weakness, confusion, dizziness, headache, difficulty swallowing, breathing difficulty, slurred speech, loss of vision, paralysis (often on one side of the body), *blackout, coma,* and death (strokes lead to death in one-third of all cases). Those who survive a stroke often suffer long-term *side effects,* including difficulties with speech and language, difficulty in moving and eating, permanent paralysis, swelling of the brain, *depression,* and uncontrollable mood swings. About a third of all strokes result in no detrimental effects.

Initial treatment for a stroke may include *drugs* designed to break up clots in the brain. Since a stroke results in dead brain tissue, surgery is usually not helpful, although it is sometimes used to unblock arteries that might cause future strokes. Long-term care for stroke patients includes hospital care and physical rehabilitation and reconditioning. Stroke victims often need to relearn how to do simple tasks such as talking, eating, and walking. Many regain the ability to take care of themselves, whereas others suffer permanent physical and psychological damage.

Sudden Sniffing Death (SSD)

A condition that results from the abuse of *inhalants*. SSD can occur when the inhaled substance takes the place of oxygen in the *lungs* and *central nervous system*. This results in suffocation and death. Inhalants can also cause sudden death by disrupting normal *heart* functioning, leading to *cardiac arrest*.

Inhalants are considered the most dangerous of abused substances. They can be found in over a thousand household products. Many stores are keeping the most commonly abused substances behind the counter. Inhalants are particularly dangerous to young children and teens because they are so easy to obtain. Nearly every inhalant can cause SSD, even if used only once.

Synergism

See also:
Polysubstance Use

The interaction of two or more *drugs* with a combined effect that is greater than their individual effects. For instance, someone who mixes a glass of *alcohol* with a single *dose* of *Valium* (both *depressants*) will experience effects several times more powerful than either of the drugs taken by itself. Synergism usually occurs with two drugs of the same class (*depressants, stimulants, hallucinogens,* etc.). Taking more than one drug at a time can easily result in *overdose* and death.

Synthetic Drug

A *drug* that is chemically produced in a laboratory rather than produced in nature. The majority of medicines today are synthetically manufactured. Synthetic drugs can be produced for less money and in greater quantities than naturally occurring drugs (those found in plants, animals, molds, and bacteria). They can also be made to duplicate natural drugs. Some are designed to produce the benefits of natural drugs without the negative *side effects*. Many illicit drugs are also synthetic, particularly *designer drugs*.

- Temperance
- THC
- Thorazine
- Tobacco
- Tolerance
- Toxic/Toxicity
- Toxin
- Tranquilizer
- Transplant
- Tricyclic Antidepressant (TCA)
- Trip/Bad Trip
- Tuberculosis
- Tuinal
- Twelve-Step Program
- Twelve Steps

Temperance

Restraint in using *alcohol* (and other *recreational drugs*). The essential idea behind the term is not necessarily *abstinence,* but rather moderation. The term "temperance," however, is often used synonymously with *sobriety.*

Temperance was a popular term during *Prohibition.* Many anti-alcohol groups promoted temperance and abstinence as the path to a healthy and moral life. Today, there is still an active temperance movement in the United States. The American Council on Alcohol Problems, founded in 1895, informs the public about alcohol-related problems as well as the consequences of drinking alcohol. Its former name was the National Temperance League.

THC

Short for tetrahydrocannabinol, THC is the active ingredient in *marijuana, hashish,* and *hash oil.* It is the chemical responsible for the *psychoactive* effects of marijuana. THC is believed to suppress activity in the hippocampus, an area of the brain that is responsible for memory, learning, and other vital life processes. THC may also destroy nerve cells in the hippocampus. Researchers are still studying how THC acts in the brain. It may function somewhat like *opiates,* and it probably increases levels of *dopamine* in the brain. A *synthetic* version of THC called dronibinol has been developed, and although it is still being researched, it is sometimes used to treat the nausea associated with *chemotherapy.*

Thorazine

The brand name of the mild *antipsychotic drug* called chlorpromazine, used to treat delusions and *hallucinations* from schizophrenia, *mania,* and other mental illnesses. It is sometimes used to treat nausea and hiccups. Like most antipsychotic drugs, Thorazine acts by affecting the levels of certain neurotransmitters (chemical messengers) in the *central nervous system.* The first antipsychotic drug, Thorazine is now used less often than it once was because it causes extreme drowsiness. Thorazine is taken orally or *injected.*

Thorazine may result in any of the following *side effects:* dry mouth, constipation, nasal congestion, blurred vision, restlessness, poor coordination, sleepiness, dizziness, *blackouts,* rash, swollen breathing passages, swollen lips and tongue, difficulty in urinating, sexual dysfunction, muscle spasms, facial tics, and *jaundice.*

An *overdose* of Thorazine may cause uncontrollable movements, anxiety, extreme dizziness, *cardiac arrhythmia,* high or low body temperature, deep sleep, blackout, *seizures, coma,* and death. While Thorazine may cause *tolerance,* it is not believed to cause *chemical dependence.*

Tobacco

Tobacco

A plant whose dried leaves are used to make *cigarettes, cigars,* and chewing tobacco. Tobacco *smoke* contains more than 4,000 chemicals, many of which are extremely harmful. Tobacco contains *nicotine* (an insecticide), tar (a *carcinogen*), carbon monoxide (in car exhaust fumes), ammonia (a strong cleanser), lead and other metals, arsenic (rat *poison*), and cyanide (a powerful poison). Other chemicals in tobacco smoke are also found in *volatile solvents, alcohol,* lighter fluids and fuels, insecticides, radioactive material, batteries, mothballs, dyes, swamp gas, rubber, and wax. Approximately forty chemicals in tobacco smoke are carcinogens. Cigarette smoking is the most common cause of *lung cancer* in the United States.

Tobacco is a *stimulant* that has no medical use and causes a long list of negative *side effects:* headaches, dizziness, nausea, vomiting, diarrhea, increased blood pressure, increased *heart* rate, cold and clammy skin, increased respiration, and breathing difficulty. Long-term side effects include chronic *bronchitis; pneumonia; emphysema;* stomach ulcers; cancer of the lung, throat, mouth, and gums; blocked blood vessels; and heart disease. *Secondhand smoke* is very dangerous to young children and can cause the same side effects listed above. An *overdose* of tobacco is nearly impossible, although the chemicals in tobacco can certainly kill when taken in high enough *doses.* Researchers have determined that smoking a single cigarette takes approximately five minutes off of your life.

Because tobacco is a popular crop in the United States, tension exists between economic interests and the anti-smoking movement.

Tobacco use can quickly lead to *physical* and *psychological dependence.* New smokers often experience nausea and headaches but quickly develop a *tolerance* for tobacco, and these side effects usually disappear with use. *Withdrawal* symptoms related to tobacco use include irritability, headache, sleepiness, hunger, and difficulty in concentrating. These symptoms can be difficult to manage for long-time smokers and often result in tobacco *relapse,* especially since tobacco is a legal product that is easy to obtain.

Tolerance

Tolerance occurs when the body becomes less responsive to a substance after it is used for an extended period of time. This development plays a large role in many instances of *addiction*. After using a particular *drug* for weeks or months, some people feel a need to use greater amounts more often to achieve the effects first experienced.

Researchers believe tolerance to drugs and *alcohol* is the result of two changes in the body that occur after prolonged use of a specific drug. First, the ability to metabolize the drug increases because of its frequent presence in the body. Second, the number of *receptors* the body has for the given drug decreases as the drug is used more often.

Resistance, a form of tolerance, refers to the condition in which the body no longer responds to the taking of a particular drug. This happens in the cases of *antibiotics* and *chemotherapy*. Physicians often decide to increase the *dosage* before halting treatment altogether or prescribing an alternate drug.

Toxic/Toxicity

Something that is toxic is *poisonous*. Toxicity refers to the extent to which something is poisonous, but it may also refer to the negative effects of a poison, *toxin*, or a *drug overdose*. Many drugs are said to be toxic substances because they have poisonous effects on the body ("toxic" is the root of the word "*intoxication*").

Toxin

A *poison* produced by a living organism, most often bacteria. An endotoxin is a toxin that remains inside the organism that produces it. These toxins can infect human beings if the organism dies and is broken apart. Exotoxins come from the surface of the organism that produces them.

Toxins can come from certain animals, such as poisonous snakes and spiders. Others come from plants, like some kinds of mushrooms.

Toxins can be countered with antitoxins, *drugs* produced from the cells of living organisms (usually horses). Many antitoxins are produced by *injecting* the toxin into a living animal, causing the animal's body to naturally create an antitoxin. These substances are then removed from the animal and used as medicine. Antitoxins may cause allergic reactions, but this is rare.

Tranquilizer

A *hypnotic-sedative* that is used to treat nervous conditions like anxiety, *mania*, manic-depressive disorder, aggressive behavior, schizophrenia, and other mental illnesses. Tranquilizers can be either *antianxiety drugs (lorazepam, meprobamate, Valium, Xanax)* or *antipsychotic drugs (Thorazine, lithium)*.

Transplant

See also:
Depressant

Transplant

A surgical process during which a diseased or malfunctioning organ is replaced with a healthy organ. The healthy organ may come from a living relative, from someone who has recently died, or in the case of tissue transplant (also called skin graft), from another area of the patient's body. This procedure is usually performed when an organ is damaged or diseased beyond repair, and the patient's life is at stake.

Organs that are transplanted include *heart, liver, kidney, lung,* pancreas, skin, cornea, hair, and bone marrow. The person who receives the transplant is known as the recipient; the source of the transplant is known as the donor. Many donors are living people, usually healthy relatives. Other donors are the recently deceased, usually those who have died in accidents.

Since the 1960s, modern medicine has come a long way toward perfecting the transplant of organs and tissue, although it can still be a dangerous procedure. Certain transplants, such as skin and cornea, are much more common and less dangerous than others, such as heart and liver transplants. Three medical advances over the last few decades have made transplants safer and more successful: immunosuppressant *drugs* that reduce the number of transplant rejections (when the *immune system* of the recipient attacks the new organ as if it were a disease); improved donor/recipient matching (blood type and other concerns); and improved surgical techniques.

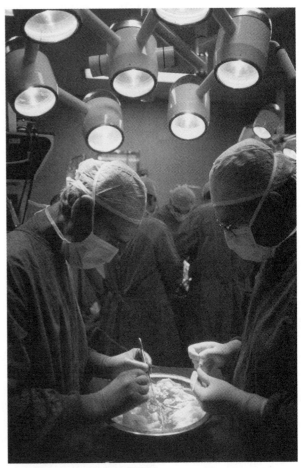

Transplants have become more successful in recent years because of advances in medicine.

Tricyclic Antidepressant (TCA)

One of the first types of *antidepressant* developed. It is primarily used to treat *depression* but has also been found to be successful in treating other illnesses, particularly obsessive-compulsive disorder (being burdened by unwanted thoughts or the compulsion to repeat certain activities).

TCAs raise the levels of certain neurotransmitters (chemicals that carry messages from one nerve cell to the next) in the brain. These particular neurotransmitters are what the body naturally uses to fight depression and other mental illnesses. It commonly takes two to three weeks for the positive effects of a TCA to set in.

Although they are among the most dependable antidepressants for mild to moderate depression, TCAs have many potentially harmful *side effects,* including weight gain, sleepiness, *hypertension,* blurred vision, dry mouth, confusion, constipation, memory loss, and sexual dysfunction. An *overdose* of a TCA can result in *cardiac arrest* and death. Because of the side effects, doctors often prescribe other antidepressants, especially *selective serotonin reuptake inhibitors.*

Tolerance and *addiction* to TCAs are rare. Most problems occur when the person fails to take a large enough *dose* or abruptly stops using a TCA. At this point, *withdrawal* symptoms may occur, including nausea, vomiting, cramps, diarrhea, chills, insomnia, and anxiety.

Trip/Bad Trip

See *Hallucinogen, High,* and *LSD.*

Tuberculosis

A contagious disease caused by the bacteria *Mycobacterium tuberculosis.* The disease, called TB for short, has been around for centuries and occurs particularly in urban areas and underdeveloped/overpopulated areas of the world. Tuberculosis is spread through the air, particularly by coughing. While cases of tuberculosis have declined over the past 100 years, it is still a problem in some countries. In America, tuberculosis has resurfaced as a complication of *AIDS.*

When contracted, tuberculosis is most often destroyed by the *immune system.* In a small percentage of cases, the bacteria can remain dormant in the *lungs* for years. Tuberculosis can then develop as a result of an impaired immune system or because of old age.

Tuberculosis begins as a general feeling of illness, including a persistent cough that produces mucus and sometimes blood. As the disease develops, the person experiences night sweats, breathing difficulty, fever, poor appetite, and weight loss. Worsening conditions include air or fluid between the lungs and the chest wall, *kidney* damage, bladder problems, painful urination, sterility, abdominal pain, arthritis, fluid in the membrane around the *heart*, enlarged neck veins, poor blood circulation, collapsed vertebrae, leg paralysis, and an infection of the brain that can lead to headaches, fatigue, nausea, *coma*, and death.

Many years ago, tuberculosis (once called consumption) often resulted in death. The development of modern prevention, diagnosis, and treatment techniques have reduced the threat, although in some countries TB is still a problem. Treatment for tuberculosis usually entails a group of *antibiotics*. Surgery is rarely necessary but is sometimes used to drain fluid from certain areas of the body or to correct damage to the spine. With proper treatment, most people recover from tuberculosis within one year.

Tuinal

A combination of *Amytal* and *Seconal*, two *barbiturates*. This *drug* is used to treat insomnia and to calm patients before surgery and dental operations. It can be taken orally or *injected*.

Twelve-Step Program

Voluntary behavior and/or *drug rehabilitation* program based on continued *abstinence* from an addictive substance and/or behavior. The success of twelve-step programs strongly depends on the individual's desire to stay *sober* (or to stop behaving in a destructive manner). Members of these programs depend on each other for support and advice. More experienced members often become "sponsors," or mentors, to the less experienced members and are called upon whenever the need arises. Twelve-step programs are considered a spiritual environment but do not prescribe any particular religion. Members are guaranteed anonymity and are usually known

Professor Albert Calmatta, bacteriologist who developed the tuberculosis vaccine BCG.

Twelve-Step
Program

173

Twelve Steps

by first names only. Some meetings are led by speakers; others are discussion-based meetings where any member can speak to the group. Twelve-step programs are often recommended by legal and medical professionals for people who have trouble breaking *addictions* to *drugs* and *alcohol,* and may be one of many rehabilitation methods the person encounters on the road to sobriety.

Alcoholics Anonymous (AA) is the original twelve-step program, established in 1935 by two former alcoholics known only as Bill W. and Dr. Bob. These two men learned that helping others achieve and maintain sobriety is an active and effective way to maintain personal sobriety. In founding AA, Bill W. and Dr. Bob established the basic principles behind all such programs. Other twelve-step programs include Narcotics Anonymous (NA), Overeaters Anonymous (OA), and Gamblers Anonymous (GA).

Twelve Steps

The following are the guiding principles on which *twelve-step programs* are based. These steps are personalized for *Alcoholics Anonymous,* but the wording differs slightly from one type of program to another.

1. We admitted we were powerless over *alcohol*—that our lives had become unmanageable.
2. Came to believe that a Power greater than ourselves could restore us to sanity.
3. Made a decision to turn our will and our lives over to the care of God as we understood Him.
4. Made a searching and fearless moral inventory of ourselves.
5. Admitted to God, to ourselves, and to another human being the exact nature of our wrongs.
6. Were entirely ready to have God remove all these defects of character.
7. Humbly asked Him to remove our shortcomings.
8. Made a list of all persons we had harmed, and became willing to make amends to them all.
9. Made direct amends to such people wherever possible, except when to do so would injure them or others.
10. Continued to take personal inventory and when we were wrong promptly admitted it.
11. Sought through prayer and meditation to improve our conscious contact with God as we understood Him, praying only for knowledge of His will for us and the power to carry that out.
12. Having had a spiritual awakening as the result of these steps, we tried to carry this message to alcoholics and to practice these principles in all our affairs.

- Valium
- Viagra
- Volatile Solvent

Valium

See also:
Antianxiety Drug

Valium

The brand name of the *benzodiazepine* diazepam, used to treat mild to moderate anxiety disorders and insomnia. This *tranquilizer* is also prescribed to treat *alcohol withdrawal, seizures,* and muscle spasms. Valium is taken orally or *injected.*

Like all *hypnotic-sedatives,* Valium causes relaxation in smaller *doses* and sedation in larger doses. In addition to alleviating anxiety disorders, Valium may result in negative *side effects,* including sleepiness, fatigue, clumsiness, slurred speech, dry mouth, blurred vision, constipation, dizziness, nausea, vomiting, cramps, rash, confusion, difficulty in urinating, *depression,* headache, *low blood pressure, cardiac arrhythmia,* sexual dysfunction, tremors, *hallucinations,* breathing difficulty, and memory loss. An *overdose* of Valium may result in sleepiness, poor coordination, confusion, slurred speech, low blood pressure, depressed respiration, *blackout, coma,* and death.

Valium can lead to *physical* and *psychological dependence* in as little as two weeks; it should not be taken for longer than four weeks. Withdrawal symptoms include insomnia, depression, cramps, muscle spasms, nausea, vomiting, sweating, tremors, and seizures. People who become addicted to Valium are not advised to quit *cold turkey;* gradual tapering off is recommended because of the potentially severe withdrawal symptoms.

Valium has a history of abuse that peaked in the late 1970s when it was a popular drug of abuse because of its ability to relieve tension and depression and make everyday problems seem less important. This drug is sometimes mixed with other *depressants* (particularly alcohol) to enhance the feelings of *intoxication.* This often results in overdose and death.

Viagra

The brand name of the *drug* sildenafil citrate, which is used to treat male impotence (inability to achieve an erection). Viagra helps to increase the flow of blood into the penis, making erection possible. This drug is designed to be used by men (primarily older men) who have trouble achieving erection. Viagra is taken orally.

Viagra

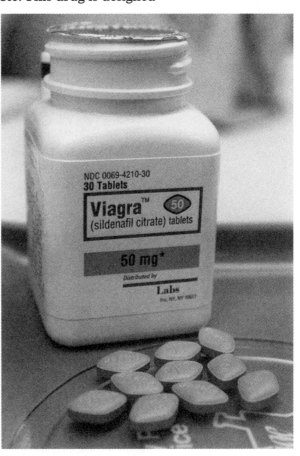

In addition to helping impotent men achieve erection, Viagra may have negative *side effects,* including headache, dizziness, rash, flushing, upset stomach, nasal congestion, diarrhea, infection of the urinary tract, disruptions in color vision, and sensitivity to light. Less common side effects may include migraine, sweating, dry mouth, nausea, vomiting, insomnia, *low blood pressure, cardiac arrhythmia, cardiac arrest, heart failure, anemia, hyperglycemia,* arthritis, tremors, *depression,* anxiety, ringing in the ears, difficulty breathing, *bronchitis, seizure,* and death (usually from *heart* complications during sexual activity). Most side effects are mild and disappear shortly after beginning to take Viagra.

Viagra should not be taken by people who have a history of heart disease. This drug has also been known to cause a condition called priapism, or prolonged and painful erections lasting four hours or more. Priapism usually happens in men who take Viagra as a *recreational drug.* Men who are capable of achieving erection without Viagra can become *psychologically dependent* on this drug when they abuse it, and they may eventually need it to achieve erections. Viagra has been abused by men who go to dance clubs and raves (all-night dance parties) because they believe it heightens the pleasure of sexual experiences.

Viagra helps to increase blood flow to the penis, making erection possible.

See also:
Club Drug

Volatile Solvent

See also:
Sudden Sniffing Death

Volatile Solvent

A type of product often misused as an *inhalant.* Volatile solvents inhaled for their *intoxicating* effects include *aerosols* (spray paint, air freshener), nail polish remover, paint thinner, butane (*cigarette* lighter fluid), propane, and gasoline. Even when used properly in a well-ventilated room, these products can produce lightheadedness in people working with them. These effects are greatly intensified when the substance is concentrated on a rag or in a paper bag and deeply inhaled (called "bagging" or "huffing").

Solvent fumes are absorbed through the tissues of the throat and *lungs* and rapidly reach the brain through the blood. Volatile solvents act as a *depressant* on the *central nervous system.* This causes breathing and *heart* rate to slow, sometimes to the point of unconsciousness. Other short-term effects may include drunkenness, floating sensation, *cardiac arrhythmia,* numbness, *euphoria,* weakness, spinning sensation, and nausea.

Volatile solvent abuse is considered to be the most dangerous inhalant abuse. After only six months of abuse, users can develop permanent damage to the organs of the body. Long-term effects can include severe brain and central nervous system damage, *liver* damage, *kidney* damage, *cardiac arrest,* lung damage, *anemia,* and bone and bone marrow damage. Some chemicals coat the lungs and prevent oxygen from entering the bloodstream. Volatile solvents can also burn the tissues of the nose, mouth, throat, and lungs. Some individuals who abuse inhalants develop a permanent tingling or loss of feeling in their extremities from nerve damage. Inhaling volatile solvents can lead to *blackout, coma,* and death, even the first time they are used.

W-Z

Wellbutrin

Wellbutrin

See *Bupropion*.

"Whip-Its"

See *Nitrous Oxide*.

Withdrawal

Caffeine withdrawal is common among individuals who give up drinking coffee.

See also:
Delirium Tremens

The physical and psychological effects experienced when a person abruptly stops using a *drug* that causes *chemical dependence*. Withdrawal occurs because the body becomes accustomed to the presence of a drug after a period of time. Sometimes the user builds a *tolerance* for the drug, resulting in the need for larger *doses*. When use of the drug is halted, the body develops *cravings* for it that manifest as feelings of physical and mental illness.

Withdrawal symptoms depend on the specific drug but may include flulike symptoms, headache, fever, nausea, vomiting, diarrhea, sweating, *depression,* irritability, anxiety, sleepiness, insomnia, decreased appetite, and weight loss or gain. Withdrawal symptoms can last from a few days to a few weeks, and in some cases for a month or longer. Withdrawal from some drugs—like *narcotics*—can be extremely uncomfortable but is not life-threatening. Other drugs—like *alcohol* and *barbiturates*—can cause life-threatening withdrawal symptoms. Still other drugs may have very mild withdrawal symptoms; *caffeine* withdrawal, for example, includes headache, fatigue, and irritability.

Xanax

The brand name of the *benzodiazepine* alprazolam, a *tranquilizer prescribed* to treat anxiety and panic disorders. On rare occasions, Xanax is used to treat pain from *cancer* (combined with *opioid analgesics*), PMS, insomnia, and *depression* (related to anxiety disorders). This drug is taken orally and may take a few days to a few weeks to begin working.

Side effects related to Xanax often occur with first use but disappear after a few days. They may include drowsiness, dizziness, poor coordination, cramps, blurred vision, dry mouth, nausea, vomiting, increased heartbeat, *cardiac arrhythmia, low blood pressure,* slurred speech, memory loss, *hallucinations,* headaches, confusion, and breathing difficulty. A Xanax *overdose* may result in sleepiness, confusion, poor coordination, *blackout, coma,* and death.

When taken for a prolonged period, Xanax can lead to *physical* and *psychological dependence. Withdrawal* symptoms usually include insomnia, abdominal cramps, nausea, vomiting, muscle cramps, sweating, tremors, and *seizures.*

Xanax

See also:
Antianxiety Drug

Zyban

Zyban

See *Bupropion*.

Where to Go for Help

Organizations

Al-Anon/Alateen Family Group Headquarters
1600 Corporate Landing Parkway
Virginia Beach, VA 23454-5617
(800) 344-2666

Alcoholics Anonymous
468 Park Avenue South
New York, NY 10016
(212) 870-3400

American Cancer Society
1599 Clifton Road NE
Atlanta, GA 30329-4251
(800) ACS-2345
http://www.cancer.org

Hazelden Foundation
P.O. Box 11
Center City, MN 55012-0011
(800) 257-7800

National Clearinghouse for Alcohol and Drug Information
P.O. Box 2345
Rockville, MD 20847-2345
(800) 729-6686

Office on Smoking and Health
Centers for Disease Control and Prevention
Mail Stop K-67
4770 Buford Highway NE
Atlanta, GA 30341
(800) CDC-1311

Hotlines

Heroin Hotline
(800) 9-HEROIN (43-7646)

Mental Health Crisis Hotline
(800) 222-8220

National Institute on Drug Abuse Referral
(800) 662-HELP (4357)

Web Sites

About.com Substance Abuse
http://substanceabuse.about.com

Alcohol and Other Drugs—Health Canada
http://www.hc-sc.gc.ca/hppb/alcohol-otherdrugs/

Alcohol and Substance Abuse
http://web.bu.edu/cohis/subsabse/subsabse.htm

D.A.R.E. America
http://www.dare.org/

Merck Manual Home Edition Online
http://www.merckhomeedition.com/home.html

National Families in Action
http://www.emory.edu/NFIA/

National Institute on Drug Abuse
http://www.nida.nih.gov/

prescriptionabuse.org
http://www.prescriptionabuse.org/

RxList—The Internet Drug Index
http://www.rxlist.com/

streetdrugs.org
http://www.streetdrugs.org/

Teen Challenge: World Wide Network
http://www.teenchallenge.com/

WebMD
http://www.webmd.com/

Bibliography

Berkow, Robert, ed. *The Merck Manual of Medical Information.* New York: Pocket, 2000.

Brecher, Edward M. *Licit and Illicit Drugs.* Boston: Little, Brown, 1972.

Burger, Alfred. *Drugs and People: Medications, Their History and Origins, and the Way They Act.* Charlottesville, VA: University Press of Virginia, 1986.

Clayman, Charles B., M.D., ed. *American Medical Association Home Medical Encyclopedia.* New York: Random House, 1989.

Goode, Erich. *Drugs in American Society.* Boston: McGraw-Hill College, 1999.

O'Brien, Robert, and Sidney Cohen, M.D., eds. *The Encyclopedia of Drug Abuse.* New York: Facts on File, 1992.

Spears, Richard A. *The Slang and Jargon of Drugs and Drink.* Metuchen, NJ: Scarecrow, 1986.

Index

A

abstinence, **2**, 33, 39, 65, 90, 141, 161, 168, 173

acetaldehyde, 13

acetaminophen, **2**, 8, 12, 42, 53, 84, 87, 91, 127, 131, 137

acid. *See* LSD.

addiction, explanation of, 2, **3**, 4

addictive personality, **3–4**, 48, 79

adrenal glands, 4, 163

adrenaline, **4**, 9, 33, 61, 70, 119

adulterant, **4**

aerosol, **5**, 178

aggressiveness, 63, 114, 171
    as result of overdose, 14
    as side effect, 9, 11, 57, 77, 119, 133, 152, 164
    as withdrawal symptom, 119

AIDS, **5**, 11, 18, 21, 90, 96, 117, 137, 164, 172

akyl nitrites, **6**, 97

Al-Anon, **6**

Alateen, 6

alcohol, dangers of, 2, 7, 8, 23, 26, 28, 43, 64, 75–76, 85, 96, 99, 109, 138, 139, 146, 160, 166, 176, 180

alcohol, definition/explanation of, **7**

alcoholics, help/treatment for, 8, 13–14, 114

Alcoholics Anonymous, 2, **8**, 64, 150, 161, 174. *See also* twelve-step programs.

alcoholism, 3, 6, 7, **8**, 14, 15, 24, 39, 87, 92, 123, 137

alcohol poisoning, **8–9**

alertness, heightened/increased, 4, 9, 31, 41, 70, 119, 125

allergic reactions, 16, 18, 50, 59, 95, 96, 98, 124, 127, 134, 142, 156, 170

alprazolam, 181

amnesia, 26, 50, 80, 103, 152

amphetamines, 6, **9**, 10, 29, 47, 57, 59, 65, 70, 119, 151, 159, 164
    effects/dangers of, 4, 6, 9, 19, 62, 85, 112, 118, 157, 165

amyl nitrite, 6, **10**, 29, 159

Amytal, **10**, 154, 159, 173

anabolic steroids, **11**, 47, 51, 63, 65, 159, 164

analgesics, 11, **12**, 20, 31, 54, 64, 70, 95, 104, 116, 127, 130, 131, 133, 135

anemia, 5, 7, 10, 11, **12**, 20, 21, 26, 87, 97, 101, 112, 124, 131, 151, 156, 177, 178

anesthetics/anesthetic, 10, **13**, 23, 24, 37, 41, 50, 56, 59, 71, 74, 77, 79, 97, 103, 108, 110, 118, 125, 126, 127, 133, 165

angina pectoris, 10

Antabuse, 8, **13–14**

antacids, **14–15**, 130, 135

antianxiety drugs, **15**, 23, 53, 79, 93, 114, 117, 171

antibiotics, **16**, 20, 26, 28, 90, 96, 104, 134, 137, 140, 170, 173

anticancer drugs, 26, 96, 104

anticonvulsant drugs, 26, 155

antidepressants, 11, **16–17**, 29, 41, 109, 120, 142, 144, 155, 160, 172

antidotes, **17**, 114, 120, 126, 138

antifungal drugs, **17–18**, 137

antihistamines, **18–19**, 44, 75, 96, 121, 156, 160

antipsychotic drugs, 8, **19**, 39, 168, 171

antivenin, 17

antiviral drugs, **20**, 21, 90

anxiety, 35, 55, 63, 72, 76, 114
    as result of overdose, 108, 169
    as side effect, 20, 24, 31, 39, 45, 56, 59, 60, 61, 70, 74, 83, 91, 92, 99, 109, 115, 116, 123, 124, 127, 142, 143, 147, 177
    treatment of, 10, 111, 117, 124, 171
    as withdrawal symptom, 9, 10, 17, 37, 53, 55, 80, 89, 93, 108, 112, 119, 120, 124, 125, 146, 152, 155, 160, 165, 172, 180

anxiety disorders, treatment of, 15, 16, 23, 24, 54, 93, 108, 110, 160, 176, 181

appetite, decreased/loss of,
    as side effect, 4, 9, 28, 36, 41, 50, 57, 88, 95, 111, 119, 123, 142, 151
    as withdrawal symptom, 11, 75, 180

as withdrawal symptom, 112
DMT (dimethyltryptamine),
61, 159
dopamine, 19, 34, 35, **61–62**, 71, 72, 79,
135, 149, 168
dose, definition/explanation of, **62**
dronibinol, 168
drowsiness,
as result of overdose, 14, 19, 89, 108,
131, 152
as side effect, 24, 28, 44, 50, 60, 74, 95,
108, 109, 124, 127, 131, 151, 156,
168, 181
as withdrawal symptom, 125
drug, definition/explanation
of, **62–63**
drug abuse, definition/explanation of, **63**
drug abuse/use, signs of, 37, 52, 63,
156–157
Drug-Induced Rape Prevention and
Punishment Act, 51
drug interaction, definition/
explanation of, **64**
drug rehabilitation, 2, 3, 4, 8, 9, 14, 35, 46,
55, 57, **64–65**, 83, 98, 107, 120,
123, 141, 144, 149, 150, 173
drug testing, **65–66**, 141
drug trafficking/traffickers, 48, 51, 53, **66**,
108, 141
drug use, stages of, **162**
dry mouth, 19, 30, 39, 42, 50, 54, 56, 59,
61, 70, 74, 89, 111, 121, 131, 142,
168, 172, 176, 177, 181
DWI, 7, 25, 27, 28, 47, **67**

E

ecstasy, 6, 10, 29, 88, 116.
See also MDMA.
electroconvulsive therapy, 55
emphysema, 28, **69**, 87, 112, 169
enabler, 44
endorphins, **70**, 129, 135, 137, 149
ephedrine, 4, 26, 52, **70**, 88, 119, 159, 161
epilepsy, 23, 24, 110, 111, 117, 154
epinephrine, 4, 127
ergot, **71**, 111
ethanol, 7
ether, 45, **71**, 77, 84

euphoria, 9, 24, 25, 40, 45, 46, 54, 56,
57, 61, 70, **71–72**, 74, 80, 83, 88,
89, 93, 95, 97, 103, 106, 114, 116,
117, 119, 120, 121, 123, 124, 125,
126, 131, 135, 138, 143, 144, 146,
149, 150, 151, 152, 154, 160, 161,
165, 178
experimentation/experimenting, 36, 63,
72, 89, 84, 133, 138, 140, 150,
161, 162

F

fatigue/exhaustion,
as result of overdose/poisoning, 37, 50,
109, 138
as side effect, 23, 45, 46, 50, 54, 83,
84, 89, 92, 117, 121, 123, 133,
165, 176
as withdrawal symptom, 9, 11, 31, 41,
112, 119, 125, 136, 150, 151, 180
FDA (Food and Drug Administration),
74, 89, 130
fentanyl, 56, **74–75**, 123, 129, 159
fermented alcohol, 7, **75**
fetal alcohol effect (FAE), 75
fetal alcohol syndrome (FAS), **75–76**
fever,
as result of overdose, 9, 29,
80, 119
as side effect, 16, 18, 19, 39, 57, 80,
111, 117, 123, 124, 126, 133, 147,
151, 164
as withdrawal symptom, 53, 75, 106,
119, 124, 180
"fight or flight" reaction, 4
flashbacks, **76**, 83, 111, 133, 143
Fleming, Sir Alexander, 134
flunitrazepam, 152
fluoxetine, 142
flushed sensation/flushing, 6, 10, 13, 30,
89, 123, 177
freebase, definition/explanation of, **77**

G

GABA, 79
gateway drugs, 72, **79**, 150
GHB, 40, 50, **79–80**, 159

ginger, 88
ginkgo, 88
ginseng, 88
glucose, 4, 98
glue sniffing. *See* inhalants *and*
    volatile solvents.
glutethimide, **80**, 146, 159

H

hallucinations, 55, 76, **82**, 89, 154, 168
    as result of overdose, 29, 57, 151
    as side effect, 9, 29, 37, 41, 42, 50, 54,
        56, 57, 59, 60, 61, 74, 88, 89, 97,
        99, 103, 108, 111, 112, 116, 118,
        119, 121, 123, 126, 133, 143, 152,
        156, 164, 176, 181
    as withdrawal symptom, 8, 37, 53, 55, 80,
        93, 112, 117, 136, 152
hallucinogens, 51, 61, 71, 76, 79, **82–83**,
    85, 90, 111, 116, 118, 126, 133,
    143, 144, 156, 157, 166
hangover, 25, **83–84**
hard drugs, definition/explanation of, **84**,
    161
hashish/hash oil, **84–85**, 107, 136, 168
hazing, **85**
headaches, 165, 173
    as result of overdose/poisoning,
        112, 138
    as side effect, 6, 10, 13, 16, 18, 20, 21, 29,
        31, 46, 54, 57, 59, 60, 74, 83, 84, 92,
        97, 108, 110, 111, 117, 121, 123, 124,
        125, 126, 142, 147, 151, 152, 155,
        156, 161, 169, 176, 177, 181
    treatments of, 11, 16
    as withdrawal symptom, 31, 106, 119,
        125, 136, 150, 152, 165, 169, 180
heart, effects of drugs on, **85–86**
heart attack, 12, 13, 20, 33, 41, 54, 58, 60,
    85, **86**, 87, 88, 92, 108, 110, 121,
    124, 164
heartburn, 14, 20, 95
heart disease/damage, 3, 7, 26, 33, 36, 69,
    86, 89, 92, 121, 131, 165, 169
heart failure, 7, 8, 9, 14, 26, 29, 33, 34,
    53, 57, 69, 76, 80, 85, 86, **87**, 92,
    99, 104, 112, 116, 119, 130, 133,
    164, 177

heart rate, inreased, 6, 9, 10, 30, 39, 40,
    41, 56, 57, 59, 70, 75, 80, 83, 85,
    89, 93, 99, 103, 111, 115, 116,
    118, 119, 124, 125, 126, 135, 147,
    169, 181
hepatitis, 7, 16, 35, 39, **87–88**, 89, 96,
    98, 101, 109, 110, 124
"herbal ecstasy," 88
herbal stimulants, 71, **88–89**, 112
heroin, 4, 17, 23, 42, 44, 47, 50, 53,
    54, 57, 75, 79, 93, 96, 98, 104,
    106, 114, 116, 118, 119, 121,
    123, 125, 129, 136, 138, 139,
    146, 149, 152, 159
    effects/dangers of, 26, 28, 84, **89**,
        112, 157
herpes, 20, 163
high, definition/explanation of, **89–90**
hippocampus, 115, 168
HIV, 5, 9, 11, 20, 21, 36, 89, **90–91**, 96,
    98, 124
homegrown, definition/explanation of, **91**
huffing. *See* volatile solvents.
hunger, 9, 46, 57, 58, 119, 147, 165, 169
hydrochloric acid, 14, 119
hydrocodone, **91**
hydromorphone, 60
hyperglycemia, 58, 98, 155, 164, 177
hypertension, 7, 10, 11, 14, 20, 21, 57, 58,
    59, 85, 86, 87, 88, **92**, 95, 110, 120,
    125, 164, 165, 172
hyperventilation, 13
hypnotic-sedatives, 15, 23, 24, 37, 50, 54,
    80, **93**, 103, 108, 111, 112, 117,
    140, 144, 146, 152, 160, 171, 176
hypoglycemia, 59, 98, 147, 155
hypotension, 110
hypothalamus, 58

I

ibuprofen, 2, 12, 91, **95**, 127
ice (crystal meth), **95**
illness, increased susceptibility to, 9
immune system, effects of drugs on, 6, 36,
    89, **96**, 119, 121, 124, 164
immunosuppressants, 96, 171
inhalants, 5, 6, 10, 29, 54, 79, 82, 85, **97**,
    112, 126, 157, 166, 178

inhibitions, loss of, 7, 50, 54, 99, 146, 152
inject/injecting,
    dangers of, 5, 9, 11, 87, 89, 90, 96, 98,
        124, 162
    definition/explanation of, **97–98**
insomnia/inability to sleep,
    as result of overdose, 116
    as side effect, 4, 9, 29, 31, 41, 52, 56,
        59, 60, 63, 70, 88, 95, 111, 119,
        120, 123, 142, 151, 155, 164, 177
    treatment of, 10, 15, 23, 24, 37, 79, 80,
        93, 108, 111, 124, 154, 160, 173,
        176, 181
    as withdrawal symptom, 10, 11, 15, 17,
        37, 53, 55, 75, 80, 89, 93, 108, 110,
        112, 120, 124, 125, 136, 146, 155,
        160, 172, 176, 180, 181
insulin, 58, **98**
intervention, 3, 35, 65, **98–99**
intoxication, definition/explanation of, **99**
irritability,
    as result of overdose, 151
    as side effect, 29, 56, 57, 83, 88, 93,
        117, 124, 152, 164
    as withdrawal symptom, 32, 47, 57, 75,
        125, 169, 180

J

jaundice, 11, 39, 87, **101**, 156, 168
jimsonweed, 126
joint, **101**, 115, 159

K

ketamine, 40, 50, **103**, 159
ketoprofen, 12, 95
kidney disease/damage, 2, 3, 14, 16, 18,
        20, 32, 39, 42, 43, 57, 58, 92, 97,
        104, 109, 119, 126, 137, 156,
        164, 173, 178
kidney failure, 36, 89, 92, 124, 155
kidneys,
    effects of drugs on, **104**
    function of, 64, **104**, 109
kidney stones, 14, 20

L

laam, 57, **106**, 121
"laughing gas." *See* nitrous oxide.
laxative, 14, **106–107**
legalization, **107–108**
Librium, **108**, 159
lidocaine, 33, **108**, 127
lightheadedness, 6, 12, 19, 37, 44, 54, 60,
        97, 115
lithium, **109**, 114, 171
liver,
    effects of drugs on, **109–110**
    functions of, 7, 39, 64, 98, 101, 109
liver disease/damage, 2, 3, 7, 10, 11, 17, 18,
        20, 32, 35, 39, 42, 43, 50, 84, 87–88,
        95, 97, 109, 110, 112, 119, 123, 124,
        126, 131, 151, 164, 178
liver failure, 88, 101, 155
lorazepam, **110**, 114, 171
LSD, 28, 40, 47, 61, 63, 71, 76, 82,
        90, 103, **111**, 117, 118, 139, 143,
        156, 159
Luminal, **111–112**, 155, 159
lung cancer, 32, 84, 112, 154, 160,
        161, 169
lung disease/damage, 3, 5, 17, 26, 28, 32,
        35, 57, 69, 97, 112, 119, 124, 131,
        133, 137, 160, 164, 178
lungs, effects of drugs on, **112**

M

"magic mushroom." *See* psilocybin.
ma huang, 70
mainline. *See* inject/injecting.
maintenance drugs, 89, 106, **114**, 118, 121,
        124
malnutrition, 9, 57, 119, 121, 133, 164
mania, 19, 29, 109, **114–115**, 142,
        168, 171
manic-depressive disorder, 19, 82, 109,
        114, 171
marijuana, 47, 53, 63, 65, 66, 72, 84, 85,
        90, 91, 101, 107, **115**, 117, 133,
        136, 139, 146, 150, 157, 158, 159,
        160, 161, 168
    effects/dangers of, 26, 28, 36, 76, 79,
        82, 84, 86, 112, 115

reverse transcriptase inhibitors, 21
Reye's syndrome, 20, 130
Ritalin, **151**, 159
Rohypnol, 40, 50, 51, 117, **152**, 159

S

schizophrenia, 9, 57, 82, 119, 133
   treatment of, 19, 39, 79,
      168, 171
secobarbital, 154
Seconal, **154**, 159, 173
secondhand smoke, 32, 86, 112, 140,
     154, 169
sedatives, 8, 93, 109, 110, 125
seizures, 43, 55, 59, 92, **154–155**
   as result of overdose/poisoning, 19, 29,
     37, 39, 42, 50, 74, 80, 89, 91, 109,
     116, 117, 119, 121, 123, 126, 130,
     131, 138, 147, 151, 169
   as side effect, 108, 109, 119, 133, 142,
     164, 177
   treatment of, 110, 111, 117, 124,
     155, 176
   as withdrawal symptom, 8, 15, 24, 80,
     93, 108, 110, 112, 117, 125, 136,
     146, 152, 176, 181
selective serotonin reuptake inhibitors, 17,
    142, **155**, 172
self-esteem, low, 3
sensory awareness, increased, 6, 10, 29, 88
serotonin, 34, 59, 71, 116, 142, 143,
    155–156
sex drive, reduced, 11
sexual assault, 25, 47, 50, 62, 152
sexual dysfunction, 19, 39, 120, 142, 155,
    168, 172, 176
sexual stimulants (aphrodisiacs), 6, 10,
    30, 88
side effect, definition/explanation of, **156**
sildenafil citrate, 177
simethicone, 15
sinsemilla, **158**
slang terms, **159**
sleep aids, 18, 19, 54, 93, 117, 130, 152,
    156, **160**
sleep disorders, treatment of, 16
sleepiness,
   as result of overdose, 30, 39, 54, 110,
     176, 181

   as side effect, 19, 23, 42, 89, 91, 108,
     110, 111, 121, 142, 147, 152, 160,
     168, 172, 176
   as withdrawal symptom, 165, 169, 180
smoke/smoking, explanation of, **160**
snort, definition/explanation
    of, **161**
sober/sobriety, definition/
    explanation of, **161**
society, reduced participation in/withdrawal
   from, 4, 35, 55, 150
sodium bicarbonate, 14, 33, 45, 71, 77
soft drug, definition/explanation of,
    84, **161**
solanine, 125
speech, slurred, 165
   as result of overdose, 37, 80, 109, 176
   as side effect, 7, 10, 15, 20, 23, 24, 54,
     93, 99, 108, 117, 124, 133, 146,
     176, 181
STDs, 20, 25, 46, **162–163**
steroids, 11, **163–164**. *See also*
    anabolic steroids.
stimulants, 9, 31, 41, 51, 56, 57, 59, 63,
    70, 88, 116, 125, 133, 144,
    164–165, 166, 169
   effects/dangers of, 6, 7, 10, 29, 45,
     85, 86, 99, 112, 119, 151, 157,
     164–165
stroke, 7, 9, 12, 26, 43, 57, 58, 59, 85, 88,
    92, 119, 133, 155, **165**
sudden sniffing death, 6, **166**
suicide/suicidal tendencies, 11, 25, 41, 55,
    83, 130, 142
sulfamethoxazole, 5
sweating,
   as side effect, 13, 39, 50, 54, 56, 57,
     60, 70, 74, 106, 111, 119, 120,
     121, 133, 142, 164, 177
   as withdrawal symptom, 53, 75, 89, 93,
     108, 110, 121, 124, 125, 136, 176,
     180, 181
swelling (as side effect), 18, 20, 24, 54, 111,
    117, 124, 127, 147, 156, 168
synergism, **166**
synthetic drug, definition/
    explanation of, 63, **166**

X

Z

Photo Credits

Acknowledgments

The editors wish to thank Marc B. Cerrone, M.D., of Day Kimball Hospital in Putnam, Connecticut, who served as an expert consultant for the manuscript.